Abolitionism: A Very Short Introduction

VERY SHORT INTRODUCTIONS are for anyone wanting a stimulating and accessible way into a new subject. They are written by experts, and have been translated into more than 45 different languages.

The series began in 1995, and now covers a wide variety of topics in every discipline. The VSI library currently contains over 550 volumes—a Very Short Introduction to everything from Psychology and Philosophy of Science to American History and Relativity—and continues to grow in every subject area.

Very Short Introductions available now:

ABOLITIONISM Richard S. Newman
ACCOUNTING Christopher Nobes
ADOLESCENCE Peter K. Smith
ADVERTISING Winston Fletcher
AFRICAN AMERICAN RELIGION
    Eddie S. Glaude Jr
AFRICAN HISTORY John Parker and
    Richard Rathbone
AFRICAN RELIGIONS
    Jacob K. Olupona
AGEING Nancy A. Pachana
AGNOSTICISM Robin Le Poidevin
AGRICULTURE Paul Brassley and
    Richard Soffe
ALEXANDER THE GREAT
    Hugh Bowden
ALGEBRA Peter M. Higgins
AMERICAN CULTURAL HISTORY
    Eric Avila
AMERICAN HISTORY Paul S. Boyer
AMERICAN IMMIGRATION
    David A. Gerber
AMERICAN LEGAL HISTORY
    G. Edward White
AMERICAN POLITICAL HISTORY
    Donald Critchlow
AMERICAN POLITICAL PARTIES
    AND ELECTIONS L. Sandy Maisel
AMERICAN POLITICS
    Richard M. Valelly
THE AMERICAN PRESIDENCY
    Charles O. Jones
THE AMERICAN REVOLUTION
    Robert J. Allison

AMERICAN SLAVERY
    Heather Andrea Williams
THE AMERICAN WEST Stephen Aron
AMERICAN WOMEN'S HISTORY
    Susan Ware
ANAESTHESIA Aidan O'Donnell
ANALYTIC PHILOSOPHY
    Michael Beaney
ANARCHISM Colin Ward
ANCIENT ASSYRIA Karen Radner
ANCIENT EGYPT Ian Shaw
ANCIENT EGYPTIAN ART AND
    ARCHITECTURE Christina Riggs
ANCIENT GREECE Paul Cartledge
THE ANCIENT NEAR EAST
    Amanda H. Podany
ANCIENT PHILOSOPHY Julia Annas
ANCIENT WARFARE
    Harry Sidebottom
ANGELS David Albert Jones
ANGLICANISM Mark Chapman
THE ANGLO-SAXON AGE John Blair
ANIMAL BEHAVIOUR
    Tristram D. Wyatt
THE ANIMAL KINGDOM
    Peter Holland
ANIMAL RIGHTS David DeGrazia
THE ANTARCTIC Klaus Dodds
ANTHROPOCENE Erle C. Ellis
ANTISEMITISM Steven Beller
ANXIETY Daniel Freeman and
    Jason Freeman
APPLIED MATHEMATICS
    Alain Goriely

Available soon:

MODERN ARCHITECTURE
    Adam Sharr
ADAM SMITH Christopher J. Berry
BIOMETRICS Michael Fairhurst

GLACIATION David J. A. Evans
AFRICAN POLITICS
    Ian Taylor

For more information visit our web site

www.oup.com/vsi/

Richard S. Newman

ABOLITIONISM

A Very Short Introduction

OXFORD
UNIVERSITY PRESS

OXFORD
UNIVERSITY PRESS

Oxford University Press is a department of the University of Oxford.
It furthers the University's objective of excellence in research, scholarship,
and education by publishing worldwide. Oxford is a registered trade mark of
Oxford University Press in the UK and certain other countries.

Published in the United States of America by Oxford University Press
198 Madison Avenue, New York, NY 10016, United States of America.

Library of Congress Cataloging-in-Publication Data
is on file at the Library of Congress.

Cataloging in Publication Control Number: 2018008019

978-0-19-021322-0

Printed by Integrated Books International, United States of America
on acid-free paper

*For educators everywhere—and especially
teachers in the Abolition Seminar.
You are truly the light of the world*

Contents

List of illustrations

Acknowledgments

This book began as a series of summer seminars for K-12 educators. Generously funded by the National Endowment for the Humanities (NEH), the seminars met for a month at a time at the Library Company of Philadelphia in 2006, 2008, 2010, 2012, and 2013. The discussions we had about abolitionism were challenging, inspiring, and often exhausting. But they were wonderful. The experience reminded me all over again of just how important the K-12 classroom is—and how much we owe educators everywhere. Sadly, we have lost some of the teachers from those seminars. But their spirit of inquiry and collegiality lives on. I'm grateful to have worked with so many bright and committed educators. It was truly an honor. This book is dedicated collectively to you!

I would like to thank several people for making the seminar and the book happen. At the NEH, Doug Arnold was my first grant administrator and a terrific help in launching the inaugural abolition seminar. Several other NEH administrators helped along the way too, making me realize just how important it is in our nation's cultural universe. Graduate students Wes Skidmore and Ben Wright made the last two seminars much better. Ben Wright also made the digital version of the Abolition Seminar a smashing success, for which I thank him profusely: www.Abolitionseminar. org. The Library Company staff was always terrific—neither the book nor the seminar would have worked without them! At Oxford, Susan Ferber was once again an amazing source of support and a tough but fair critic. The book is better and shorter for her sharp eye. At home, Lisa Hermsen kept me going through thick and thin and always offered a smile after a long day at the computer. You too, Snoopy!

Introduction: Abolitionist agitation in a world of slavery and pain

A few years before he died in 1895, the great African American leader Frederick Douglass predicted that it would take a very long time for the world to appreciate the abolitionist movement. An escaped slave who played every conceivable role in the abolitionist struggle—editor, orator, organizer, political strategist, Underground Railroad operative, and military recruiter during the Civil War—Douglass knew that abolition played a key role in destroying Atlantic slavery, the most powerful economic and political institution of early modern society. Indeed, without abolitionist activism, slavery might well have survived into the twentieth century.

Were Douglass to return today, he would be glad to learn that abolitionists, slave rebels, and race reformers are celebrated in gleaming TV documentaries and award-winning books. Not since the nineteenth century have abolitionists been so visible.

Of course, Douglass would be troubled by the persistence of racism. Like many reformers, Douglass believed that abolitionism was a dual movement, one aimed at destroying both bondage and racial prejudice. Moreover, he understood that abolition was a global movement of reformers trying to navigate the color line as would-be equals. Seeing everything from educational inequality to the alarming rise in black incarceration in contemporary America, Douglass would be sad that abolitionism remains an unfinished movement.

But he would not sit idly by. In fact, Douglass would say one simple thing: keep fighting. "If there is no struggle, there is no progress," he proclaimed in 1857 at the height of sectional debates over slavery. People who wanted to see freedom and justice reign but did not "agitate," he continued, "want crops without plowing." For Douglass and countless others, activism was the keynote to abolitionism. Whether they were Caribbean slave rebels or pacifist preachers in the U.S. North, abolitionists constantly fought for slavery's destruction and a new brand of human equality. We live in a world they helped make—an imperfect one, to be sure, but a very different one from that which they inherited.

This book offers a brief survey of abolitionism. While I focus mostly on Anglo-American reformers in the eighteenth and nineteenth centuries, the book surveys Atlantic-wide movements that began with slave rebels in the 1500s and ended with Brazilian emancipation in the 1880s. Wherever it took shape, abolitionism was both a meditation and a movement: a meditation on "big ideas" about freedom and equality and a complex movement of people, organizations, and events designed to bring those ideas to fruition. While scholars have learned much about slavery and freedom during the past several decades, they have often veered away from seeing abolitionism as a social movement—an activist struggle akin to the civil rights movement in the twentieth century. Douglass knew better. As he noted again and again, abolitionism was about agitation. As readers will see, I view abolitionists as agitators and change agents, not merely moralists and pious perfectionists. In an era charged by Black Lives Matter, environmental justice struggles, and #MeToo, the story of abolitionist agitation remains highly relevant and timely.

Abolitionism 101: Who, where, how, why?

In thinking about abolitionism, we might begin with a very basic question: wasn't slavery going to end anyway? More than a century after slavery's global demise, it is easy to take abolition for granted. For a good part of the twentieth century, both popular writers and mainstream American historians saw abolitionists as a nuisance more than anything. For them, slavery's demise flowed from big economic shifts, particularly the rise of free labor regimes that made bondage inefficient. In the United States, "Lost Cause" scholars also argued that southern masters were benevolent and likely would have allowed slavery to perish had not maniacal abolitionists pushed them to disunion and Civil War. Disturbingly, this revisionist view has appeared in some twenty-first-century guises: As Andrew Delbanco has argued, abolitionists may have meant well but they pushed too hard and led the nation toward a ruinous war. Forgetting about the centuries of black blood that underwrote slavery in the first place, neo-revisionists wonder if abolitionist agitation was effective or worthwhile.

Yet as former slave John Sella Martin noted after the Civil War, it would be a mistake to take abolitionism for granted. "I know this," he told global reformers in Paris in 1867, abolition was "won" through the hard struggles of rebels and reformers, not granted by slaveholders and their supporters. Martin argued that enslaved people were the first abolitionists. Motivated by freedom dreams, they sought to break "the chains of bondage" from Saint-Domingue to the U.S. South. They gained crucial allies through time and space—fellow agitators who broadened abolition's reach and scope. But nothing came easy to abolitionists.

As the world's first social movement, abolition was something new under the sun. Abolitionist ideas and actions reframed how people understood slavery, race, global freedom, and multicultural democracy. When English writer Samuel Johnson published his famous dictionary in the 1750s, there was no entry for "abolition" or even "slavery." Eighty years later, Noah Webster's American dictionary had entries on "abolition," "slavery," and "manumission"—terms commonly used by abolitionists to raise consciousness about bondage. "Emancipation," Webster's 1828 dictionary noted, was the "act of setting free from slavery, servitude, subjection or dependence" entire classes of people, such "as the emancipation of slaves by their proprietors" or governmental abolition programs. In fact, Webster noted that "slavery no longer exists in Great Britain['s mainland]...[or] in the northern states of America"—a reality made possible by abolitionist activism. As Ira Berlin, Steven Hahn, and others have noted, abolition was a lengthy process and it started when both enslaved people and their allies challenged slavery's regular standing in the Atlantic world.

They had much to overcome. As recent historians have shown, slavery remained a dominant economic and political institution for much of the nineteenth century. From Britain to Spanish Cuba to the U.S. South, slave regimes prospered and even expanded. The British "slave lobby" stalled abolitionist legislation in Parliament for years. On the other side of the Atlantic, American slavery doubled in size every few decades and the United States became the world's largest slaveholding nation by 1860—containing roughly four million enslaved people, or nearly twice the number in Brazil and Spanish Cuba combined. American slavery was worth more than banks and railroads combined in the antebellum era while slave-derived crops such as cotton dominated U.S. exports and generated enormous wealth for northern insurers, banks, and trading companies. Today, the aggregate value of slavery (from enslaved people themselves to slave-derived goods) would probably exceed the worth of many top global companies, including Apple and Amazon. Even if U.S. masters embraced compensated emancipation in 1860—as did Great Britain and France earlier—the going rate for enslaved people (which exceeded $1,200 for what was known as a prime field hand by the Civil War era) would have cost nearly as much as Union expenditures during the entire Civil War.

From France to Brazil, the story was much the same: slavery brought wealth to nations, cities, and people. It also brought untold—and unfathomable—misery to enslaved people everywhere. A world without abolitionists demanding change would have been very different indeed.

So, who was an abolitionist? A transatlantic cause, abolitionism was less a single movement and more a series of allied struggles that coalesced around slavery's destruction. The award-winning scholar Manisha Sinha has recently written that anyone who aided "the slave's cause" was a kindred spirit, a generous definition many abolitionists would support. But as the movement expanded, some abolitionists—particularly black people—argued that reformers had to fight equally hard for racial justice. Strategic discussions over black equality often divided abolitionism, making clear that not all activists saw the movement in precisely the same way.

Defining just who was an abolitionist, and who made the most difference, can be tricky. Who was more important, emancipating statesmen like Lincoln or slave rebels in Saint-Domingue? Both presided over massive emancipations in the Atlantic world; neither belonged to formal antislavery organizations. Were those who did belong to formal abolition societies less important than Lincoln or slave rebels? While these are difficult questions, they remind us that abolitionism was a continuum of activists and reformers. Movements by their nature are diverse and require diverse types of agitators to succeed. I define an abolitionist as any person, group, or political party for which slavery's destruction became the central aim. Merely thinking about slavery could be defined as the start of the start of an abolitionist journey. But the commitment to ending bondage truly made someone an abolitionist. And that meant that statesmen, rebels, and reformers all had a place in the movement.

Abolitionists joined the movement for many reasons. Enslaved people and free blacks struggled for personal liberty while their allies were motivated by religious, humanitarian, and/or social values. Some abolitionists believed in biblical commands to aid "the least among us" while others were humanitarians inspired by new rights-related discourses that appeared in the Enlightenment era and the Age of Revolution. Where previously it had been rare for people to sympathize with the plight of others, by the early 1800s it was not strange to see reformers who worried about "suffering humanity." A change in human perception, as several scholars have noted, allowed humans to see each other as essentially equals and thus committed to the collective betterment of society.

Abolitionism was also part and parcel of a major communications revolution that allowed ever-more people to learn about, and join, the burgeoning movement. From slave narratives that uncovered the terrible truth behind bondage to antislavery newspapers that discussed the movement's goals and ideas, abolitionists utilized media in stunningly modern ways. They were ahead of their time.

Abolitionists and human rights

Whatever motivated them to join the struggle, abolitionists across time and space returned to a core principle of democratic modernity: people could not be treated as things. What is slavery, a British abolitionist asked in 1846? It was not unfair economic relationships, the reduction of political privileges, or even "restraints on freedom" (problematic thought these things were). If that were true, the very idea of government, family, and work would be enslavement. Rather, Atlantic bondage was a formal legal condition that turned "persons into things." "Enslaving men [and women] is reducing them to articles of property"—that is slavery's "intrinsic, unchanging element." This meant that masters were "not robbing a man of his privileges but of himself!" Slaves were "bartered, leased, mortgaged, bequeathed, invoiced, shipped," all out in the open and with the support of law.

Even children and grandparents became chattel, or movable property. Harriet Jacobs, whose pathbreaking autobiography

Incidents in the Life of a Slave Girl (1861) uncovered the particular horrors that female slaves endured, wrote that her master "told me I was his property; that I must be subject to his will in all things," including sexual domination. "My soul revolted against the mean tyranny. But where could I turn for protection?" She realized that every black person she knew, from enslaved children to grandparents, was treated as "property." That was a horrifying thought. Securing bodily freedom was thus at the top of abolitionists' agenda.

Abolitionists also ushered in new concepts of human rights that extended understandings of freedom and equality. For once slaves had been liberated, abolitionists asserted, they were to be made "persons" before the law, meaning that they had common claims to political rights, civic personhood, and protection under the law. Slaveholders denied each of these things to enslaved people, thus nullifying an essential part of democracy itself. "The claim to hold property in man destroys the very idea of right" and thus rights, William Lloyd Garrison noted before the Civil War. In fact, the concept of human property "exterminates human society." Slavery was modern democracy's enemy; there was no such thing as human rights as long as slavery persisted. In routing French masters, Haitian slave rebels claimed the rights of revolution and constitution making. They then founded a nation whose constitution banned bondage forever.

For abolitionists, human rights were universal and could never be relinquished. "[W]e hold human rights to be inalienable," a black abolitionist asserted in a remarkable article from *The Colored American* in 1837, "because moral qualities are indelible; because the human soul is immortal." Indeed, "[w]e claim them... not as rich men, or as poor men, not as learned or unlearned men... not as 'men of property and standing.'" Rather, he said in conclusion, "we claim them on the ground of our common human nature.... Not because we are Americans, or Europeans, or [Asians] or Africans" but because we are human beings.

Movements for political and social change necessarily focus on key concepts to gain public support: "rights and liberties," "justice," "freedom from oppression." The abolitionist cause was successful precisely because it mobilized people across time and space on behalf of these core principles. A century apart, British reformer Thomas Clarkson and Brazilian abolitionist Joaquim Nabuco agreed that slavery violated the essential tenants of modernity and that enslaved people had human rights.

Yet as recent scholars have reminded us, social movements also elide alternate ideas about liberty. One cultural corollary to abolitionism was the focus on the educational and cultural uplift of former slaves in Western society—the idea that they needed to be lifted not only out of bondage but also from a degraded status. That language framed black freedom as a potential problem: if African people did not meet the norms of civilizing Western nations, emancipation might fail. Ibram X. Kendi has called this "uplift suasion," and he reminds us that it reflected the dominant society's values while overlooking former enslaved people's concerns with power and autonomy. Similarly, James Sweet has noted that Atlantic dissidents like Domingos Alvares, an African man who liberated himself from bondage in colonial Brazil in 1739 and dedicated his life to healing others from the pain of slavery, were unconcerned with economic or cultural uplift. It is a good reminder for anyone studying the abolitionist movement.

Indeed, we should not romanticize abolitionists. They were fallible human beings who aimed high but often fell short of their own lofty goals. They also stumbled on issues relating to race, gender, politics, and leadership. Black activists criticized white reformers as racially insensitive, women protested men's myopia in not supporting their egalitarian struggles, and runaway slaves and kidnapped free blacks often defended their right to use violent tactics when others argued that all race reformers should embrace pacifism. Like many reformers, abolitionists (black as well as white) could be preachy, self-righteous, and dramatic. The image of the suffering and often insufferable saint has some merit.

Abolitionism agitators and the triumph of reform

Yet it is equally important to remember that abolitionists helped take down the pain-making institution of slavery, thereby allowing Atlantic people to focus on other issues like equality and civil rights. "There could be no Civil Rights Movement," the historian James Oakes has trenchantly argued, "until there was no more slavery." Like Douglass, Oakes asks that we never forget what abolitionists were up against or what they accomplished.

Take the domestic slave trade in the United States, a highly profitable business that abolitionists tried to stop for decades.

1. Abolitionist Jesse Torrey used this striking image of the domestic slave trade in his book *A Portraiture of Domestic Slavery, in the United States* (Philadelphia, 1817). As avenging angels appear overhead, a slave coffle is marched by the U.S. Capitol building during the War of 1812. Torrey argued that slavery tarnished the "splendid fabric—of freedom."

Even in Washington, DC, one could see slave coffles throughout the early 1800s. Think about it: near the present-day National Museum of African American History and Culture, people of African descent were legally (and publicly) bought and sold. "One would think that slavery and the slave trade were the last things to have…in the capital of a boasted free nation," one abolitionist handbill angrily commented. "But there they are." In 1817, abolitionist Jesse Torrey made that outrage visible to people who might never get to Washington. The irony of that fact and the anger it aroused was movingly conveyed in his engraving of a coffle of enslaved people passing by the Capitol building. Finally, in 1850, abolitionist campaigns convinced Congress to eradicate the slave trade in Washington. It was a small but crucial step on the road to full freedom.

This is precisely what generations of abolitionists did: fight against the injustice of slavery and racial oppression. We can never know enough about their struggles to change an ugly and painful world.

Chapter 1
Early abolitionism: Prophets versus profits

Who was the first abolitionist? Well before an organized abolitionist movement took shape in the eighteenth century, some brave person challenged slavery. We know that because slavers themselves discussed the resistance of captives. Perhaps the first abolitionist was a slave rebel in the earliest years of the Middle Passage. Perhaps it was someone who evaded capture along the West African coast.

The first abolitionist may have been Native American. No sooner had imperial slavery taken shape in the Americas than indigenous people challenged bondage. Spain's earliest colonial ventures in both the Caribbean and South America targeted Native people as would-be slaves, provoking fierce opposition. Their resistance struck religious dissidents like Bartolomé de las Casas, a Spanish monk who published scathing rebukes of Native enslavement in the sixteenth century. By the 1670s, Spanish monarchs issued abolition decrees in Chile and Peru undercutting Native bondage. The great Quaker abolitionist Anthony Benezet much admired de las Casas, modeling his activism on the monk's efforts.

Benezet was also inspired by African battles against enslavement. As Europeans turned from Native to African labor, he and others noted, black resistance followed. Among the first documented slave rebellions was a 1522 uprising of captive Africans in the

2. Scholars estimate that revolts occurred on at least 10 percent of Atlantic slave-trading voyages. This French image, from a book on sailors' experiences, depicts revolt as a not-so-distant reality of the Middle Passage.

Spanish Caribbean. A century before the landing of twenty Africans in Virginia, slave resistance was already etched into the historical record.

Slave resistance shadowed the expansion of Atlantic slavery. Surveying records from roughly 36,000 voyages, scholars now estimate that roughly 10 percent of slave trading vessels experienced a revolt. African resistance increased the cost of slaving voyages by requiring more crew members and costlier insurance, thus cutting into profits. This reduced the overall number of transatlantic voyages and prevented the potential enslavement of several hundred thousand people. Thus, while we may never know their names, the first global abolitionists were enslaved people who struggled against a new and more intractable form of human bondage.

Slavery's profits versus abolitionist prophets

African people inspired wider attacks on Atlantic bondage. Motivated by religious beliefs, including biblical injunctions to obey the Golden Rule and avoid "man-stealing," these new allies of enslaved people helped put abolition on the Atlantic world's political and cultural radar during the late 1600s and early 1700s. Soon, the first formal abolition societies appeared in London, Philadelphia, and Paris, and antislavery networks connected activists from the Caribbean to West Africa to North America.

No matter where abolitionists appeared, they had to overcome the accumulated weight of proslavery theology, economics, and politics. In a famous book , historian David Brion Davis argued that abolitionists were "up against" a system of economic and psychological mastery with ancient roots as well as modern cachet. Unfree labor systems proliferated from ancient Rome to Africa, and Christianity, Judaism, and Islam offered theological rationales for the enslavement of nonbelievers, debtors, and war captives ("just slaves"). On the philosophical front, notable thinkers from Plato and Aristotle onward had sanctioned classic slavery.

Yet abolitionists also squared off against a new type of bondage in early modern society. As European empires built New World economies based on mining wealth (including gold and silver in the Caribbean and South America) and much-desired cash crops—sugar, coffee, indigo, rice, cotton, tobacco—they created massive labor needs. Neither indentured servants from Europe nor indigenous people could keep pace. In turning to captive

African labor, imperial masters transformed slavery itself into a terrible institution of near-complete human domination.

Indeed, slavery shifted drastically in size and scope. Though a pan-African slave trade had operated for centuries—with Muslim and Arab traders transferring several million people from Central and West African locales to the Middle East and Mediterranean Europe—the transatlantic slave trade created an even bigger forced population transfer. Between the 1400s and the late 1800s, approximately 12 to 15 million people of African descent endured the Middle Passage. Portuguese traders brought captive Africans into Lisbon well before Christopher Columbus's famous voyages. After the Spanish joined the fray, transatlantic slaving ventures heralded a lucrative future for European nations. Soon British, French, Dutch, American, and even Scandinavian nations participated in the international slave trade.

New World slavery spread across a vast geographical terrain. The overwhelming majority of enslaved people went to South American and Caribbean locales; a much smaller number arrived in North America. Wherever captives went, they followed the insatiable demands of a rising international market for slave-derived commodities. Unlike traditional bondage, New World slavery was very much an economic affair.

Unlike classic bondage too, New World slavery became linked exclusively to race. Racialized slavery did not appear immediately, and there were variations among imperial regimes. Still, New World masters increasingly tagged people of African descent as slaves. During the 1660s, colonial assemblies in Virginia and Maryland linked slave status to African or black people. This racial marker allowed masters to better control servile populations. Race further redefined New World slavery by making bondage perpetual through a person's bloodline. In classic slaving systems, bondage stopped at one's death; now

it devolved to one's children, their children's children, an
on until a formal legal document (known as a manumissi
liberated enslaved people.

New World enslavers went to such lengths for one very simple
reason: slavery was a moneymaking machine. From the
colonial American South to the Caribbean, slaves produced
enormous wealth for masters and investors alike. Tobacco
saved the earliest Virginia settlements from disaster while rice
plantations generated tremendous fortunes for South Carolina
gentlemen. The French colony of Saint-Domingue was known
as the "Pearl of the Antilles" for its lucrative sugar plantations.
By the 1780s, the death rate skyrocketed, though French
masters simply increased African imports to fuel the
plantation furnace.

Slavery was not monolithic. In British North America, small
proprietors utilized African labor to build colonial settlements
and economies. Ben Franklin owned five slaves during his lifetime,
never releasing any of them, and they all helped run either his
business or his household. In Boston, Newport, New York, and
Baltimore enslaved people ran households, did arduous daily
chores, and aided merchants. In rural areas, enslaved people
sowed crops, built barns, tended livestock, and cleared forests
for settlement and development. Slavery was central to American
dreams large and small.

To say that abolitionists had a nearly overwhelming task is an
understatement. Whether in North America, Great Britain,
France, or Greater Spain, slavery was the engine driving Atlantic
development.

Before they could do anything else, then, abolitionists had to
label slavery a problem. That task began with enslaved people's
challenges to bondage, which compelled new groups of allies
to step forward on their behalf. These early reformers sought

o ameliorate slavery's harshest aspects. In Spain, religious
authorities urged the Catholic Church to protect enslaved people
from abusive masters. Some reformers went further, supporting
a policy known as *coartación*, which allowed enslaved people to
work part of the week and save money for self-purchase. As a
result, free black communities grew in many Spanish colonies.
By 1800, one-sixth of Spanish Cuba's population was comprised
of free blacks.

Similarly, some English reformers began urging better treatment
of enslaved people. Led by the Society of Friends ("Quakers"),
they argued that all human beings contained God's "inner light."
As children of God, they argued, enslaved people should be
treated more humanely and given access to the Christian gospel.
This proto-abolitionist step envisioned slavery as morally wrong,
helping foster further alliances between enslaved people and
Quakers.

Abolitionist Friends

Unsurprisingly, Quakers issued the first formal challenge to
bondage in colonial America: the Germantown Protest. Adopted
in 1688 by a small band of German émigrés outside Philadelphia,
it called bondage a sin and asked fellow Quakers to follow the
Golden Rule: treat others as you wished to be treated. "Is there
any that would [want]...to be sold or made a slave for all the
time of his life?" the document asked. Written by Daniel
Pastorious and signed by just three other men, it was forwarded
to Quaker meetings but not acted upon.

Nevertheless, the Germantown Protest became a model of
antislavery witness for subsequent generations. As religious
dissidents, Quakers had been oppressed by the Church of England
and then by American Puritans—they knew social stigma.
After listening to enslaved people's complaints, some Quakers
critiqued their friends and family as hypocrites. In 1737,

Benjamin Lay, who saw bondage's horrors in Barbados before moving to Pennsylvania, castigated Quaker masters in a pamphlet entitled "All Slave-keepers...Apostate." The next year, he splashed berry juice on members of a Quaker meeting to symbolize the blood on the hands of slaveholders. Though less dramatic, New Jersey Quaker John Woolman roamed the mid-Atlantic countryside on a truth-telling mission about slavery's sinful nature. These consciousness-raising activities led to Quaker emancipation policies: the banning of slave trading within the Society of Friends in 1759 and the banning of slaveholding itself in 1776.

Quaker activists soon expanded their outreach to mainstream society. Their efforts were well-timed. Enlightenment ideas about rationality, virtue, and noble sentiment allowed abolitionist ideas to gain cachet among learned men in politics and law. No figure became more influential than the Quaker schoolteacher Anthony Benezet. Based in Philadelphia, Benezet was a formidable activist, publicist, and networking agent who constantly worked to broaden the abolitionist cause. Viewing media as the key means of mobilizing reformers across Atlantic society, he published numerous pamphlets condemning the international slave trade, colonial slavery, and European treatment of both Native Americans and Africans. Few people came away from Benezet's pamphlets unmoved. He also launched a school for people of color to prove that blacks had the same abilities as whites. His death in 1784 prompted one of the largest funeral processions in Philadelphia. Notably, it included African Americans.

Among Benezet's transatlantic allies, none proved more valuable than Granville Sharp. A London shopkeeper, Sharp read Benezet's works and agreed that slavery was both a religious sin and a social evil. Sharp also saw the British court system as an instrument of liberation for enslaved people. With the slave trade enriching British merchants, investors, and ship captains, captive blacks were shuttled in and out of London, Manchester, and Liverpool. Taking advantage of these urban settings, they ran away and sought abolitionist allies like Sharp, who began representing them in courts.

Sharp scored a major victory for abolition in 1772 when he successfully sued for the freedom of a runaway slave named James Somerset. Seeking sanctuary from his abusive Massachusetts master while in London, Somerset prevailed upon Sharp to take his case to court. Presented with evidence of slavery's abuses, the judge, Lord Mansfield, decreed that bondage could not be tolerated on the liberty-loving English mainland. The Mansfield decision liberated as many as 15,000 enslaved people (though not those in the colonies).

The Mansfield case inspired more concerted abolitionist action in England over the next two decades. Both former slaves and white reformers coalesced into a loose network of abolitionists who sought to mobilize opposition to the slave trade. In the early 1780s, they mobilized an impressive public relations campaign against the captain of the *Zong*, who tossed overboard 132 captive Africans to allegedly save his crew from starvation during a stormy slave-trading voyage. After the captain claimed restitution from an insurance company, a former slave named Olaudah Equiano approached Sharp about fighting back. Equiano believed that the *Zong* affair might prompt a public outcry and spur the abolitionist cause in England. Sharp and Equiano shamed the captain, compelling the insurance company to deny his claim.

As both the Mansfield and *Zong* cases showed, Great Britain served as a key base of operations for black as well as white abolitionists. Equiano, Quobna Ottobah Cugoano, Ignatius Sancho, and others exploited Britain's cultural and legal resources—an open press culture, an increasingly sympathetic judiciary, and prominent allies—to fight slavery. Like Equiano, they often utilized autobiography to raise awareness about slavery's violent realities. Equiano's narrative, published in 1789, provided heart-rending accounts of his kidnapping, the Middle Passage, and his desire for freedom. Showing that he had the same emotions, fears, and dreams as any human being, he challenged the hypocrisy of slaveholding. "O, ye nominal Christians!" he wondered, "might not an African ask you... [why we are] torn from our country and friends, to toil for your luxury and lust of gain?" As lecturer, author, and activist, Equiano sharpened abolitionism's moral focus and sense of purpose.

The British struggle took another step forward in 1783, when abolitionists submitted their first petition to Parliament against the slave trade. Four years later, they founded the Society for Effecting the Abolition of the Slave Trade (SAEST) in London. Headed by Quakers, the group included Sharp and star Cambridge student Thomas Clarkson, whose "Essay on the Slavery and Commerce of the Human Species" (1785) riveted reformers for its depiction of slavery as the philosophical foil to English liberty. The crusade against the slave trade attracted other notable supporters too, including poet Hannah Moore, renowned producer of ceramics Josiah Wedgwood, and parliamentarian William Wilberforce. Wedgwood produced one of the enduring symbols of the transatlantic abolitionist movement: a medallion with a kneeling slave asking, "Am I Not a Man and A Brother?" Though British efforts against the slave trade were stymied in Parliament, that phrase became a rallying cry for generations of Anglo-American abolitionists.

Abolitionism in the Age of Revolution

The Age of Revolution vastly expanded abolition's reach, as statesmen, philosophers, and egalitarian reformers scrutinized slavery as a violation of natural rights. Revolutionary movements stretching from the newly independent United States to France to the Caribbean pictured bondage as out of step with emerging republican institutions and made equality the watchword of Western modernity.

Enslaved people helped usher in the Age of Revolution. In Tacky's Rebellion of 1760, perhaps as many as a thousand Jamaican slave rebels attacked British masters on hundreds of plantations. Though suppressed, the uprising was widely reported across the Atlantic world and spawned copycat rebellions against British authority. In the opening salvo of the American Revolution, colonial Americans began referring to themselves as "slaves" to the British—rebels who wanted "liberty or death," in Patrick Henry's famous phrase.

As the colonial crisis with Great Britain intensified, enslaved people used revolutionary rhetoric to push abolitionism into the public sphere. Deploying the language of liberty against American masters, they argued that people of color had legitimate claims to freedom and justice. In 1773, a quartet of enslaved Bostonians petitioned the colonial legislature for black liberty. In 1776, enslaved people in Charleston, South Carolina, boldly marched in public for their liberty. In Salem, Massachusetts, former slave Caesar Sartar published a searing newspaper article challenging Americans to live up to their revolutionary language by emancipating bondsmen and women everywhere.

During the war, African Americans compelled both American and British forces to consider broader emancipation policies. In November 1775, British general Lord Dunmore undercut the strength of American patriots by issuing the first emancipation proclamation of the age. Dunmore's proclamation declared that any enslaved person fleeing to British lines in Virginia would be liberated. A few years later, the Philipsburg Proclamation provided freedom to enslaved people reaching British lines in the northern theater of war. Though scholarly estimates vary, between twenty thousand and sixty thousand enslaved people fled to the British and staked a bold claim to freedom.

Not to be outdone, American patriots attacked slavery as anathema to the new cause of freedom. The Declaration of Independence, authored in 1776 by America's leading slaveholding philosopher Thomas Jefferson, imagined a world where equality was a self-evident truth and slavery a thing of the past. While some slaveholders thought Jefferson went too far, others believed that the Declaration expressed America's highest ideals. A host of statesmen professed hatred of slavery during the Revolution. Before he signed the Declaration, Pennsylvania's Benjamin Rush called for the abolition of the slave trade, while after 1776 the radical pamphleteer Thomas Paine argued that slavery itself must be vanquished. Alexander Hamilton, John Adams, Roger Sherman, Gouverneur Morris, and many other revolutionaries saw bondage as a glaring contradiction to American ideals.

South Carolinian John Laurens proposed mobilizing black troops as a way to defeat the British and expand American liberty. The scion of a slave-trading family, he urged state and federal officials to offer enslaved people freedom in exchange for military service (masters would be compensated too). Although Laurens died before his plans took shape, other states utilized black soldiers, often with freedom as a lure. The First Rhode Island Regiment, a segregated unit comprising more than two hundred African Americans (including many enslaved people who gained their freedom by enlisting), remains the most famous example. But a tradition of interracial activism also emerged during the war, as black militiamen fought alongside whites at Lexington, Bunker Hill, and Boston. Overall, roughly 5,000 African Americans served in the American military during the war.

Why did blacks support the patriot cause? James Forten, a free black teenager in Philadelphia, volunteered for the American navy after hearing the Declaration of Independence read publicly. Forten argued that the Declaration justified his claims to equality and justice. Similarly, Lemuel Haynes, a mixed-race minister from

Connecticut who fought at Bunker Hill, identified with the revolutionary cause of justice. Like Forten, he saw African Americans as the new nation's moral conscience.

No figure seemed more important in this regard than Crispus Attucks. A former slave who was killed by British troops at the Boston Massacre on March 5, 1770, Attucks assumed a mythical importance among whites as well as blacks for standing on the front lines of American freedom. During the nineteenth century, black writers reminded Americans that Attucks had delivered the "first blow for liberty," as black historian William C. Nell famously put it. For Nell, the American Revolution was inherently a civil rights struggle.

Abolitionist activism after 1776

By the late eighteenth century, the abolitionist movement had matured on several fronts. In the religious sphere, Anglo-American reformers deployed a wide range of biblical arguments against bondage to counter masters' proslavery claims. Inserted in essays, handbills, and images, and early slave narratives, they became talking points in the transatlantic movement. Abolitionists noted that Exodus 21:16 condemned both slavery and the slave trade in the harshest terms: "He that stealeth a man and sell him...shall surely be put to death." Similarly, in Leviticus 25:10–11, masters were enjoined to "proclaim liberty throughout all the land" every fifty years. Acts 17:26 heralded the equality of humans by noting that the Almighty had "made of one blood all nations of men." Citing Exodus 10:3–4, both black and white abolitionists also warned New World slaveholders to remember that God had already destroyed Egyptian slaveholders for failing to heed Moses' plea: "Let my people go."

On the political and institutional front, abolitionists took a major step forward by creating organizations dedicated to the sole cause of emancipation. Inspired by the burst of civic activism spawned by the American Revolution, statesmen and reformers from across the social, religious, and political spectrum came together in abolition societies that lobbied for antislavery action in both government and society. Led by principled men who believed that slavery violated not only Christian ethics but also revolutionary doctrines of liberty, these organizations often included notable citizens, particularly in the North. John Jay and Alexander Hamilton joined the New York Manumission Society (NYMSS) while Ezra Stiles, the president of Yale, became president of the Connecticut Abolition Society. The Pennsylvania Abolition Society (PAS) was led by Benjamin Franklin and then Benjamin Rush—both signers of the Declaration of Independence. Abolitionist groups also took shape in New Jersey, Rhode Island, Delaware, Maryland, and even Virginia. By the 1790s, so many groups existed that reformers launched a biennial national meeting: the American Convention of Abolition Societies.

No group was more important than the PAS. The world's first antislavery society, it was founded in 1775 and then reorganized after the Revolution. In 1787, it codified abolitionism by forming a constitution and bylaws that assigned specific tasks to committees and working groups, allowing activists to work simultaneously on goals ranging from black education to abolitionist outreach in the Atlantic world. As an incorporated entity, the PAS had a legal status in the state of Pennsylvania that allowed people to give charitable donations to the antislavery cause. And it had a public listing in the Philadelphia business directory.

Like other groups, the PAS agitated for abolitionist laws in the new nation. After 1776, bondage remained legal in every American state except Vermont, whose constitution banned slavery. Abolitionists argued that slavery blemished the American character and gave lie to the nation's Revolutionary War promises. "It is our duty," one member of the NYMSS observed, "both as free citizens and Christians . . . to endeavor, by lawful ways and means, to enable [slaves] to share equally with us, in that civil and religious liberty … with which an indulgent providence has blessed these [United] States."

Nevertheless, because they were led by men of property and standing, early abolition groups often opposed immediate emancipation. Favoring gradualism, abolitionists believed that slavery must be dismantled slowly, thus doing justice to masters as well as enslaved people. Early abolition societies in the United States did not formally admit black members, which limited their strategic outlook. Indeed, many white reformers agreed that property rights must be balanced against human rights.

The major exception to this rule was Massachusetts, whose Supreme Court declared slavery unconstitutional in 1783. The court responded to freedom suits brought by black litigants and white lawyers. Both Elizabeth Freeman (known as Mum Bett) and Quok Walker ran away from abusive masters, found abolitionist allies, and went to court for their freedom. In Freeman's case, Theodore Sedgewick, who became a corresponding member of the PAS, argued that slavery violated the state's constitutional guarantee of equal rights. Chief Justice William Cushing agreed, telling the jury that the Massachusetts constitution "is totally repugnant to the idea of being born slaves." While masters fumed, nearly two thousand enslaved people were liberated.

Elsewhere, abolitionists found that gradual emancipation appealed to non-slaveholders as well as masters, especially in states with larger populations of enslaved people. By century's end, five northern states adopted gradual abolition schemes. Pennsylvania (with roughly seven thousand slaves) was the first, passing a law in March 1780 that liberated enslaved people born after the act at age twenty-eight. Connecticut and Rhode Island (each contained fewer than six thousand slaves) followed suit in 1784, while New York—which more than twenty thousand slaves—debated various gradualist proposals before passing one in 1799. New Jersey (with more than ten thousand slaves) became the final state to embrace gradual abolition in 1804. In each case, state abolition laws established penalties for scofflaws, pressing down on masters' property rights. In Pennsylvania, masters who did not register slaves with justices of the peace might lose their human property. Moreover, visiting politicians and businessmen had a grace period of only six months before they had to comply with the law. Beyond gradual abolition, reformers pushed for laws against slave trading and kidnapping.

Despite its gradualist foundations, northern abolition gave rise to sectional divisions over slavery. In fact, black and white abolitionists used "free soil" principles to isolate slavery in politics and law. By prosecuting slave traders in various northern ports, suing those who kidnapped free blacks from northern cities and towns, and representing fugitive slaves in northern courts, abolitionists sought to strip away slavery's operability above the Mason-Dixon line. The PAS, whose legal aid system helped hundreds of African Americans, made Pennsylvania a haven for people of color throughout the mid-Atlantic region. In one case from the 1790s, a Virginia mistress claimed the children of an enslaved mother who fled to Philadelphia. PAS lawyers argued that the children were born in Pennsylvania and had to be registered according to the state's abolition law. Having failed to do that, the Virginia woman forfeited claims to them. As one PAS lawyer observed, they were "lucky to have been born in Pennsylvania." With such decisions in mind, early abolitionists searched state and federal laws for precedents and loopholes that might hamper bondage's operation nationally and put in on a path to destruction.

Abolition and the U.S. Constitution

Despite such hopes, early American abolitionism remained a limited movement, especially in the South. Many slaveholders refused to support even gradual abolition, no matter their moral qualms. In Virginia, respected jurist St. George Tucker failed to gain legislative approval of a gradual abolition plan despite some masters' philosophical opposition to slavery. In South Carolina, North Carolina, and Georgia, masters saw slavery as an economic necessity and did not apologize for it. Either way, gradual abolition threatened the white social order in states with large slave populations. Instead, private emancipation became southern blacks' best legal route to freedom. Virginia eased restrictions on private emancipation in 1782, prompting between six thousand and ten thousand manumissions over the next several decades. Yet this paled next to slavery's growth in the Old Dominion.

The Federal Constitution of 1787 challenged abolitionism by hewing to slaveholders' concerns. While it created a national government and aspired to build "a more perfect union"—a potential boon to abolitionists—the Constitution also protected bondage in several ways. It guaranteed masters the right to reclaim fugitives "from service" across state lines, which allowed Congress to pass the first fugitive slave law in 1793. It prevented congressional passage of a national slave-trading ban for twenty years, which allowed South Carolina alone to import forty thousand captive people. And in its most notorious section, the Constitution counted three-fifths of a state's enslaved population to calculate its seats in the House of Representatives. The three-fifths clause provided what scholar Paul Finkelman has called "political muscle" to the South. Without the clause, Pennsylvania would have had a higher number of House seats because its free population exceeded Virginia's (431,000 to 404,000). Yet by counting three-fifths of Virginia's nearly three hundred thousand slaves, the Constitution gave the Old Dominion more congressional representatives. Little wonder that southerners could successfully push for the admission of new slave states in the early 1800s and fend off efforts to repeal the three-fifths clause. Moreover, because the Electoral College was tied to congressional representation, Virginia and other southern states

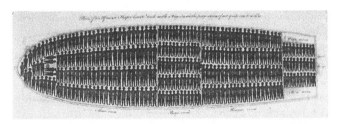

3. This depiction of a slave-trading vessel illuminated the inhumane conditions of the Middle Passage. Distributed by the nation's leading abolition society before 1800—the Pennsylvania Abolition Society—it was part of a transatlantic campaign to end the slave trade.

had additional power in presidential contests too. Unsurprisingly, Virginia sent four of the first five presidents to the White House.

Beyond these provisions, the Constitution symbolized the importance of sectional compromise, further limiting abolitionist attacks on southern slavery. Where many northern states adopted manufacturing and free labor principles, most southern states remained tied to cash-crop agriculture and slavery. A nation of divergent interests required constant compromise, even northern politicians believed, to avert disunion.

Abolitionists learned this lesson when they petitioned the first federal Congress in February 1790 to "step to the very verge of the powers vested in you" to eradicate the slave trade and perhaps slavery itself. Like British reformers, the PAS sought to mobilize public sentiment against the slave trade by distributing disturbing images of the Middle Passage. In 1789, it circulated a graphic rendition of an average "African ship" that "crowded" hundreds of people below deck. As anyone could see, these conditions were simply inhumane. The group hoped that Congress would agree. Yet Deep South masters were enraged, threatening disunion if abolition guided national policy. The memorial was buried in committee. In subsequent petition campaigns, abolitionists toned down their rhetoric and focused on lesser measures (such as preventing Americans from trading slaves to foreign nations). The lesson: American abolitionists had to overcome political fears about disunion as well as proslavery arguments about bondage's economic importance. Once again, abolitionists learned that they were up against a lot.

Abolitionism at one hundred

In the century since four antislavery Quakers had signed the Germantown Protest, abolitionism had developed into an organized movement with a coherent agenda, transnational centers of operation in London and Philadelphia, and a pantheon of recognizable reformers. Drawing strength from religious teachings, slave uprisings, international wars, black protest, and revolutionary philosophy, abolitionism put bondage on the defensive in Atlantic society—a nearly unthinkable thing a century earlier. Focusing on the rights of enslaved people and the injustice of slaveholding, abolitionists became known as change agents who were willing to agitate for emancipation in both political and social venues.

And yet, abolition's first century also showed that slavery was a thoroughly resilient institution that would not go away easily. To end bondage, abolitionists would have to keep agitating.

Chapter 2
The rise of black abolitionism and global antislavery struggles

As a new century loomed, black activists pushed abolition forward across the Atlantic world. The greatest example came in Saint-Domingue, where a slave rebellion in the 1790s compelled the French government to issue a broad emancipation decree. A more assertive brand of abolitionism also developed in the United States as free black communities rebuked American statesmen for allowing racial oppression to prosper. Former slave Richard Allen used the death of George Washington to issue a stirring appeal for national emancipation that was printed by newspapers in Baltimore, New York, and Philadelphia. Noting that Washington had crafted an emancipation will that would free slaves after his wife's death, Allen challenged American slaveholders to follow the great man's lead. Just as Washington liberated slaves to "wipe off the only stain" on his character, so too must Americans eradicate wickedness in their midst to avert eternal damnation.

While other important abolitionist initiatives took shape during the late 1700s and early 1800s, African people's rising activism became a hallmark of the age.

4. A revered black abolitionist, Richard Allen purchased his freedom and founded both Mother Bethel Church in Philadelphia and the African Methodist Episcopal (AME) denomination. Even after his death in 1831, he remained a hero to black and white abolitionists.

Saint-Domingue

In August 1791, enslaved people went to war against colonial masters in Saint-Domingue. While slavery's brutality prompted the uprising, the rebellion also flowed from the French Revolution, which promised universal rights to all citizens. The revolt followed unsuccessful protests for equality by free people of color, who imbibed revolutionary currents too. After their protests were violently quashed, enslaved people rebelled against colonial authority, holding off local militias and then French forces. As the rebellion expanded, it terrified slaveholders across the Atlantic world.

The revolt inspired twin emancipation proclamations. Hoping to end the rebellion, French officer Léger-Félicité Sonthonax banned slavery in the colony in 1793. A member of the small but influential French abolitionist movement that had formed in the 1780s (as "Les Amis de Noirs," or the friends of the blacks), Sonthonax heeded enslaved people's demands by banning bondage at once. In February 1794, the French National Assembly outlawed bondage throughout the empire. From Saint-Domingue to Martinique to Guadeloupe, roughly seven hundred thousand enslaved people were liberated. Thus, the grandest emancipation edict of the eighteenth century flowed from a slave rebellion.

Caribbean slave rebels exploited demographic trends to fight the French. In Saint-Domingue, blacks outnumbered whites by 10 to 1. In the United States few areas had such powerful black majorities. Moreover, slave rebels successfully combined violent means with political ends, claiming the revolutionary tradition of rights and liberties as their own. Toussaint Louverture, a former slave who gained freedom in the 1770s and became one of the uprising's leading figures, depicted the slave revolt as a modern republican rebellion against tyranny (and not merely a servile war against whites). Deploying the language of the French Revolution against masters, he joined with enslaved people in demanding universal liberty. So skillful was Louverture that he even managed to get U.S. president John Adams to engage in diplomatic exchanges and trade relations with rebels.

Many others sought to bury Louverture's army. English and Spanish forces tried unsuccessfully to invade the island while U.S. slaveholders opposed any recognition of the slave rebels. Thomas Jefferson, who called slave rebels "cannibals," repudiated Adams' pro-rebel trading policy after becoming president in 1800. In France, Napoleon Bonaparte tried to retake the island but was foiled. His only success was the capture of Toussaint Louverture, who died in a French prison. Nevertheless, in 1804, slave rebels established Haiti, the Western Hemisphere's first black republic.

The new nation banned bondage forever, making it a standard bearer of freedom for African people everywhere and an outlier among Atlantic nations. In the United States, Haiti haunted slave masters for generations to come. Who would be the next Toussaint Louverture, slaveholders wondered?

As Gabriel's Rebellion in Virginia illustrated, American masters were right to worry. Named for enslaved leader Gabriel, who planned an uprising in Southampton County in the summer of 1800, rebels sought to march on the state capital of Richmond and kidnap Governor James Monroe to compel the passage of a state emancipation law—much like Dominguan slave rebels had done. Tellingly, rebels promised not to harm antislavery Quakers, Frenchmen, or Methodists. A massive rainstorm washed out the uprising, however, and the rebellion was soon betrayed from within. Several dozen conspirators were tried and executed, including Gabriel, who refused to explain the plot. Black Virginians learned that violent uprising was difficult, if not impossible. While Gabriel hoped to persuade whites to back emancipation (or else), the uprising compelled many whites to crack down on black freedom. By 1806, a new Virginia law restricted private emancipation.

Still, both Haitian independence and Gabriel's Rebellion illuminated the potential power of black insurgency. In Gabriel's Virginia, some masters recognized that slavery was an inherently problematic institution even as they condemned the rebellion. Indeed, both Jefferson and Monroe considered colonizing blacks overseas as a way to rid the Old Dominion of slavery and African Americans. More broadly, slave rebels like Gabriel and Toussaint

entered the pantheon of black heroes who led resistance to
oppression in the Atlantic world.

Slave revolution also created intense debates among transatlantic
abolitionists about violent means. Was slave rebellion justified?
Many white abolitionists believed that uprisings were
counterproductive. Counseling patience among enslaved people,
they called on masters across the Atlantic world to enact gradual
abolition laws that would preempt slave rebellion.

American Quaker John Parrish was not so sure. Having agitated
against bondage for decades, Parrish wondered whether white
reformers had the right to tell oppressed blacks what to do. As he
noted in a private essay in the early 1800s, if the sin of slavery—"man
stealing," in his eyes—continued unabated in the Atlantic world,
then slave revolution might well be justified. Yet even Parrish
stepped back from publicly sanctioning a black uprising, urging
American politicians to embrace emancipation before more slave
rebellions occurred.

Black abolitionism in the United States

African Americans saw the slave uprising in Saint-Domingue as
a call to action. "My brethren," Boston's Prince Hall observed in
a 1797 pamphlet, "let us remember what a dark day it was with our
African brethren, six years ago, in the French West Indies. Nothing
but the snap of the whip was heard, from morning to evening.
Hanging, breaking on the wheel, burning, and all manner of
tortures, were inflicted on those unhappy people." "But," he
continued, "blessed be God, the scene is changed." African Americans
had to imbibe the lessons of Saint-Domingue by pushing harder
for abolition and racial equality in the United States.

As Hall's words indicate, African Americans created a powerful
nonviolent counterpart to the uprising in Saint-Domingue.
Eschewing violent tactics—free blacks constituted less than

10 percent of the overall American population and usually no more 5 to 20 percent of many northern urban populations—they fought an ideological war against racial oppression in the public realm. Arguing that slavery and segregation violated the American creed of liberty and justice for all, black abolitionists issued moral missives aimed at the American conscience. Though prevented from running for political office and (in many cases) voting, they used books, pamphlets, speeches, newspaper articles, and petitions to make their case. In this first golden age of black protest, African Americans produced more than 1,800 printed documents by 1830.

The power of the black voice stemmed from its communal foundations. By the early 1800s, African Americans had established a host of reform institutions that faced both inward (toward communal benevolence and philanthropy) and outward (toward political activism). In 1780, the black community in Newport, Rhode Island, launched the Free African Union Society, which supported benevolent activities and uplift initiatives. In 1785, Bostonian Prince Hall founded the first black Masonic Lodge. In 1787, Philadelphia reformers established the Free African Society (FAS), which aided distressed African Americans and fought for civil rights, including the protection of black burial grounds. In New York City, Baltimore, Richmond, and even Charleston, free blacks formed religious, philanthropic, and educational groups, often with an abolitionist edge.

Indeed, these institutions anchored generations of black protest. The first sit-in occurred in Philadelphia when Richard Allen and Absalom Jones challenged segregated seating at St. George's Methodist Church. Although African Americans had been attending the church in increasing numbers, white parishioners objected to equal seating in the House of the Lord. Church elders placed blacks in the back of the church or directed them to a new balcony. During one service, Allen and Jones ignored the policy and sat in the main pews. When asked to leave, they refused. After prayer, they led an exodus of black congregants.

They established the first black churches in Philadelphia: Allen's African Methodist Episcopal (AME) Church and Jones's African Episcopal Church of St. Thomas. Soon there were African Baptist and African Presbyterian Churches too. Here and elsewhere, black churches merged faith and social protest. In Allen's case, the AME denomination came into being after blacks sued for institutional freedom from white Methodists, who had claimed Allen's church building. In 1816, the Pennsylvania Supreme Court sided with Allen. After joining with other black Methodists who wanted to be free from white control, the AME denomination was born. By the Civil War, it became perhaps the largest black-controlled institution in the United States.

Allen and Jones's struggles were not unique. In Baltimore and New York, black worshippers protested against segregated churches, while in New England African Americans battled segregated schools. As racial inequality became the norm in many emancipating northern locales, black communal institutions served as a launching pad of opposition. Heeding the words of biblical Psalm 68—"Princes Shall Come Out of Egypt; Ethiopia shall soon stretch out her hands unto God"—blacks saw themselves as a rising people who would redeem African identity and American society through prophetic protest. Only when they were free would America be a true land of liberty.

Reared in churches and communal groups, a generation of black writers condemned slavery and racial inequality as moral stains on American society. In Baltimore, Daniel Coker published a mock dialogue between an "African minister" and a Virginia planter that shredded proslavery rationales. One of the few black pamphlets of protest issued below the Mason-Dixon line, Coker's 1810 work flowed from conversations at Bethel Church, where his congregation had already challenged both segregation and slavery.

Now Coker challenged masters in the heart of slave country to embrace emancipation.

Allen and Jones had already issued a similar challenge. After a yellow fever epidemic nearly wiped out the nation's temporary federal capital of Philadelphia in 1793, black leaders volunteered to aid the suffering city and prove that African Americans were valuable citizens. Though honored by the mayor, blacks were criticized in a popular history of the epidemic. Written by printer Matthew Carey, the book claimed that many African Americans had plundered white homes and charged high fees for nursing services. Allen and Jones issued a righteous rebuttal: "A Narrative of the Black People during the Late Awful Calamity in Philadelphia" (1794). Arguing that African Americans had risked their lives when many whites, including Carey, fled the city, they castigated anyone who saw blacks as disturbers of the peace. In a separate essay, Allen claimed that slavery spawned Carey's racist claims. Allen's abolitionist appeal urged Americans to liberate blacks and treat them as civic equals.

When Jones petitioned the federal government in 1799, he found that few politicians saw free blacks as citizens. Asking that blacks be allowed to "partake of the Liberties and unalienable Rights" in the Constitution, Jones's memorial sought a congressional crackdown on the overseas slave trade. As one Deep South representative scolded his colleagues, the memorial was meaningless because blacks could not be citizens. Congress rejected Jones's memorial by a vote of 84 to 1. Yet because northern papers reported on the matter, Jones's left a historical footprint for later generations to see.

Slave trade abolition and the second slavery

Despite Jones's setback, global abolitionism took a key step forward in the early 1800s when several European and American nations banned the slave trade. Norway, whose ships were responsible for roughly 1 percent of the Middle Passage during the 1700s, banned the trade in 1802. The British Parliament followed suit with a law in March 1807. The U.S. ban took effect on January 1, 1808. This flurry of slave-trading bans flowed from abolitionist agitation, which shamed those nations that did not outlaw the barbaric trade. Indeed, worried that France and other countries would resume slave trading after the Napoleonic Wars, British abolitionists circulated petitions demanding that Britain prioritize slave-trading bans at the Congress of Vienna in 1815. Pushed by the British, seven nations, including France, Portugal, Spain, and the Netherlands, pledged to support the "Universal Abolition of the Slave Trade." It seemed like a new era.

Slave trade abolition inspired a new wave of transatlantic activism. Hoping to stop the flow of slaves to Cuba and Puerto Rico, Spanish abolitionists reprinted British anti-slave-trading documents. Even after Spain signed a bilateral treaty with Great Britain in 1817 to curtail the trade above the Equator, slaving activity continued. In 1825, Barcelona activist Agustín de Gimbernat sought to reinvigorate the cause by translating Thomas Clarkson's celebrated pamphlet, "The Cries of Africa." As de Gimbernat observed, Spaniards should be "horrified" to know anyone "so depraved" as to be a slave trader. It would take many more years—and more agitation—to completely stop Iberian slave trading.

Beyond the slave trade crusade, both enslaved people and free blacks used independence struggles in Latin American countries to undermine New World bondage. In Peru, independence brought a wave of freedom claims from enslaved people who supported the anti-Spanish cause. Even wives of black soldiers claimed that they had aided Peru's freedom struggle and thus deserved liberty. Similarly, in Venezuela, thousands of people of African descent helped colonial rebels defeat Spain, exacting freedom in the process. As Simón Bolivar, who belatedly supported emancipation as a war measure, asserted, it was crazy to think that a "revolution for freedom" could "maintain slavery."

A slaveholder himself, Bolivar manumitted roughly one hundred slaves and supported his new nation's abolition law of 1823 that liberated children of slaves. Though it would not be finalized until decades later, Venezuela's emancipation law was part of an abolitionist wave, as Chile, Central America, and Mexico would pass similar (or even more stringent) emancipation laws.

Nevertheless, slavery proved to be a resilient institution in the nineteenth century. Indeed, a "second slavery," as scholars refer to it, developed in the Spanish Caribbean, Brazil, and the U.S. South. Based on new products (such as cotton) and new markets (sugar from Cuba), slavery remained a key part of the transatlantic economy. Ironically, Saint-Domingue helped fuel the second slavery, as British, Spanish, and even American sugar producers filled the void left on the world market.

American slavery's economic vitality was also tied to geographic expansion. The purchase of the Louisiana Territory in 1804 without major antislavery restrictions opened the fertile trans-Mississippi River valley to the cultivation of sugar, cotton, and other staple crops. Although some abolitionists and slaveholders argued that these new territories would dilute slavery—a policy known as diffusion, where whites moving west into small farming settlements would reject slavery as costly and inefficient—many planters saw the Southwest as a lucrative region that would revivify bondage. Despite a massive slave rebellion in Louisiana Territory in 1811—in which rebels carried copies of the French "Declaration of the Rights of Man"—several new slave states came into the national fold: Louisiana (1812), Mississippi (1817), and Alabama (1819). Early abolitionist gains were nearly wiped out by slavery's southwestern growth.

Investment in slave-derived products boosted the national economy. Northern bankers, insurers, and investors joined slaveholders in backing new southern ventures. The numbers told the tale: By the 1830s, the slave population surpassed two million—almost triple the number in 1790—and cotton and sugar became staple American exports. Worse, between 1800 and 1860, nearly one million black souls were sold on the domestic slave trade. Some northern masters sold enslaved people south to avoid gradual abolition laws while some Upper South masters sold excess captive laborers "down the river" to recoup financial investments.

Slavery's economic importance underscored the surging political power of masters and compelled abolitionists to think more deeply about their alliances with northern politicians. When territorial Missouri applied for statehood in 1819, many northerners opposed the admission of another slave state even though they did not favor southern emancipation. Abolitionists tried to exploit antislavery feeling by petitioning against Missouri's admission and speaking in favor of territorial restrictions on slavery. But they also realized that antislavery politicians—men who opposed bondage's expansion but never committed to broader abolitionist programs—were not committed emancipationists.

In the case of Missouri, abolitionists learned that compromise was still a powerful part of national politics. When slaveholders refused to back down from territorial restrictions on bondage, politicians engineered an artful compromise to end the stalemate: Missouri entered the Union as a slave state while Maine (peeled off from Massachusetts) entered as a free state. Congress prohibited bondage in western territories above the 36°30' parallel, excluding Missouri, but not below it. Indeed, abolitionist attempts to prohibit slavery from territorial Arkansas, which was under the control of the federal government, had already failed because slaveholders saw it as fertile ground for bondage.

Abolitionists claimed victory in the Missouri Compromise, but they lost much. By conceding slaveholders' rights in certain parts of the west, they had done little more than reassert the importance

of the Northwest Ordinance of 1787, which limited slavery's
growth in the Great Lakes region. Moreover, antislavery statesmen
ultimately agreed with slaveholders that union trumped abolitionist
concerns out west. Finally, the Missouri Compromise showed that
a new generation of southern slaveholders saw abolitionism—and
not slavery—as the nation's enduring problem. Defending bondage
more aggressively, they condemned even moderate abolitionists as
troublemakers set on destroying the union.

Black protest redux

Making matters worse, established abolition societies suffered
from a leadership crisis when a succession of elder activists passed
away. By the 1820s, Benjamin Rush, Warner Mifflin, John Parrish,
and others were gone.

African Americans stepped into the leadership void. Using
communal institutions as a base, they offered powerful new
critiques of the domestic slave trade, northern race relations,
and slaveholders' renewed power in a republic supposedly
dedicated to liberty. To highlight slavery's alarming resurgence,
black abolitionists held annual New Year's Day commemorations
of the ending of the slave trade. Though advertised as celebrations
of America's slave-trading ban, these January 1st events became
strident abolitionist forums. Black leaders attacked slavery's
growth and vilified politicians who ignored the domestic slave trade.

According to Philadelphian Russell Parrott, the slave-trading
ban of 1808 had been only "a partial abolition." Only
when Americans secured "the emancipation of those already in
bondage" would the "triumph of philanthropy... be complete."
New Yorker Andrew Simkins noted in 1810 that American
politicians were duty-bound to stop the domestic slave trade, which
replicated the horrors of the Middle Passage by tearing apart
African American families and spreading bondage into new
parts of the American Union. Turning impassioned speeches

into trenchant essays, black pamphleteers further spread the abolitionist gospel of January 1st commemorations. Until full freedom occurred, these writers made clear, black bodies everywhere would be constantly at risk, whether from kidnapping threats in the North or the domestic slave trade's explosive growth in the Deep South.

The formation of the American Colonization Society (ACS) in 1816 intensified black abolitionists' concerns. Supported by prominent slaveholders, including Bushrod Washington and James Madison, the ACS urged masters to manumit slaves, who would then be compelled to leave the United States. By connecting emancipation to black expulsion, and compensating masters along the way, the ACS sought to undercut slavery and export America's race problem in one fell swoop. Some Upper South slaveholders saw the ACS as a proto-abolitionist group that wisely promoted voluntary manumission over government-mandated emancipation schemes, thus circumventing the thorny issue of masters' property rights. Despite much hype, the ACS did not achieve anything close to its lofty ambitions: between 1817 and 1867, it sent roughly 15,000 blacks to the ACS's West African settlement of Liberia (which achieved independence in 1847). Meanwhile, slavery's population doubled again.

The ACS divided the abolitionist ranks. Though some reformers supported the group, many white abolitionists saw colonization as a costly and impractical program that would never lead to national emancipation. Many African Americans opposed the ACS as a Trojan horse designed to remove free black agitators from the United States. They also saw colonization as a reverse Middle Passage that would forcibly separate families with firm roots on American soil. Although African Americans had themselves flirted with colonization since the Revolutionary era, they often emphasized elective affinity as the key to emigration. Like other Americans, they hoped to leave and return to the United States on their own terms.

The ACS's appeal among northern whites further concerned black abolitionists. With auxiliary societies in Massachusetts, Ohio, and Pennsylvania, the ACS illuminated the rise of racial tensions above the Mason-Dixon line. As free black communities expanded in the wake of emancipation laws, northern whites expressed increasing fear of black economic competition in the workplace and targeted black festive culture as an intrusion on "their" civic space. In New England, whites satirized black emancipation festivals and slave trade celebrations while in Philadelphia and New York white artists developed new cartoon genres that poked fun at African American aspirations in politics and society. The first example of black minstrelsy in American song probably came from a white New Yorker who parodied blacks' belief in equality during the War of 1812. Even white abolitionists conceded that race relations had reached a nadir.

As the ACS's popularity grew, so too did anti-black sentiment. Even frustrated black leaders who once considered colonization as an alternative to American oppression changed their tune. From Richmond to Pittsburgh, black communities staged angry demonstrations against the ACS. The most famous meeting occurred in Philadelphia in 1817, when several thousands gathered at Richard Allen's Mother Bethel Church to register their dissent. In a follow-up pamphlet, free black leaders proclaimed that they would never separate from enslaved people and would fight for abolition and racial justice within the United States.

Over the next fifteen years, free blacks pushed back against the ACS. In public meetings, pamphlet literature, orations, and newspaper articles, they argued that colonization was inimical to the abolitionist cause. As one Pittsburgh activist argued, "We are freemen...we are brethren...we are countrymen and fellow-citizens, and [we are] as fully entitled to the free exercise of the elective franchise as any men who breathe." As Richard Allen put it more famously in 1828, African Americans had helped

build America, watering the soil with "our tears and our b
They deserved nothing less than freedom and equal citiz

David Walker

Influenced by African American struggles for justice, new
generations of white as well as black reformers would castigate
the ACS and call for a revitalized abolitionist struggle capable of
vanquishing both southern slavery and northern racism. No black
activist was more influential in this regard than David Walker.
Born free in North Carolina, he eventually moved to Boston
and ran a used clothing shop on the waterfront, mingling with
black sailors and dockworkers who spread news of egalitarian
struggles around the Atlantic world. After joining the Boston
General Colored Association, a communal institution dedicated
to black uplift, he became a fierce opponent of the ACS and
encouraged black people everywhere to fight militantly for
freedom and justice.

A brilliant writer, Walker envisioned print media as a conduit to
the black masses. His 1829 pamphlet, *Walker's Appeal*, channeled
the anger pulsing through black Atlantic communities. A
visionary work of protest, the *Appeal* went through several
editions and circulated widely. Walker had copies of the pamphlet
sewn into black sailors' clothing, urging them to pass it along to
free blacks as well as enslaved people at various ports. He also sent
stacks of the pamphlet to free blacks in the South, asking them to
sell it cheaply or give it away. White authorities found copies of
the *Appeal* in several southern states. In Virginia, the General
Assembly conducted a "confidential" investigation of the
subversive pamphlet and cracked down both on black literacy
and on the circulation of antislavery literature.

While aimed at blacks, Walker's *Appeal* also addressed whites.
Walker condemned colonization and slavery in harsh terms and
called slave rebellion a justifiable response to racial oppression.

See your Declaration Americans!!!! Do you understand your own language?" he lectured white readers. In case they did not, he printed the key words in capital letters: "ALL MEN ARE CREATED EQUAL!!" In passages like these, Walker raised the volume of the abolitionist struggle. Even after his death in 1830—from consumption, though his allies suspected foul play— Walker remained a black abolitionist icon.

Abolitionist media

Without a doubt, Walker drew inspiration from black resistance across the Atlantic world. Yet his rise also reflected important shifts in transatlantic media. During the 1820s and 1830s, the cost of both paper and printing technology decreased while improved transportation networks facilitated the diffusion of literary productions globally. Everyone from reformers to merchants joined the communications revolution.

For the first time, abolitionists had their own newspapers. While Tennessee Quaker Elihu Embree's short-lived publication *The Emancipator* (1820) was the first, Benjamin Lundy's *The Genius of Universal Emancipation* became the most successful abolitionist paper of the decade. Launched in 1821, it covered a range of topics: slavery's expansion in the Southwest, the rise of anti-abolitionist sentiment, and the appearance of new antislavery groups like the Free Produce Society (which eschewed slave-produced goods). Published variously in Tennessee, Ohio, Pennsylvania, Maryland, and Washington, DC, Lundy's paper became essential reading for abolitionists.

British reformers followed Lundy's lead with the publication of *The Anti-Slavery Monthly Reporter* in London. Inaugurated by Zachariah Macaulay in 1825, the paper served as a clearinghouse for Atlantic abolitionism. Highlighting the rise of abolitionist petition drives, antislavery discussions in church and government venues, and debates over unfree labor throughout the empire, the paper celebrated a new age of abolitionist agitation. Even those opposed to abolition agreed that reformers' embrace of media made the movement formidable. As one critic charged, the key "tools" of the abolitionist "war" on slavery in the nineteenth century included "newspapers, pamphlets, periodicals, tracts, books, novels, essays." From Great Britain to the United States, abolitionists used printed communications to mobilize "the entire moral forces of the human mind" against slavery.

The advent of *Freedom's Journal* in 1827 may have been the most important development in abolitionist media. Published in New York City, it was the first newspaper owned and edited by African Americans. "We wish to plead our own cause," the paper's inaugural editorial proclaimed. "Too long have other spoken for us. Too long has the public been deceived by misrepresentations, and things which concern us dearly." While *Freedom's Journal* survived only two years, it circulated among white as well as black reformers and heralded the rise of new African American reformers. Just as black luminaries like Richard Allen contributed to its columns, so too did emerging figures like David Walker, who distributed and wrote for the journal.

The paper's founding editors were also rising figures in black abolitionism: Presbyterian minister Samuel Cornish and the Caribbean-born educator John Russwurm. They championed black history and celebrated African and African American achievement. But their eyes were always on the prize of black freedom. As the paper's masthead declared, "righteousness exaltalth a nation." The lesson from Proverbs (14:34) was clear: The United States must embrace emancipation or face eternal condemnation.

Cornish and Russwurm eventually had a falling out—with Russwurm emigrating to Liberia to overcome American race prejudice—but not before *Freedom's Journal* made a splash on the abolitionist scene. As black abolitionists had predicted, they would rejuvenate the antislavery struggle by speaking truth to power and not backing down from slaveholders or their allies. *Freedom's Journal* became the model for a succession of black-run newspapers over the next several decades, and it served as a reminder that African Americans would remain antislavery visionaries.

Chapter 3
The time is now: The rise of immediate abolition

Organized abolitionism had been in operation for nearly fifty years when it took a radical turn during the 1830s. A new generation of Anglo-American abolitionists made immediate emancipation the movement's standard, spawning wide-ranging debates about abolitionist radicalism. Led by a diverse and multicultural constellation of activists, abolition's second wave embraced a crusading brand of reform that refused to defer to slaveholders' or politicians' concerns. Experimenting with new tactics—from mail campaigns that bombarded slaveholders with antislavery literature to physical defenses of fugitive slaves—abolitionists became full-time activists and professional reformers. It was an explosive era of activism.

Radical black protest and British abolitionists

Second wave abolition was framed by black rebellion. Major slave revolts occurred in Louisiana (1811), Spanish Cuba (1812), and the British Caribbean (Barbados in 1816 and Demerara in 1823). Many younger abolitionists saw these uprisings as a call to radical action. In 1822, after former slave Denmark Vesey's uprising was betrayed in Charleston, South Carolina, a wave of southern blacks migrated north to avoid violent reprisals (Vesey and several other conspirators were executed). Morris Brown, a Vesey confidant, found sanctuary at Richard Allen's Church in Philadelphia, where he relayed stories of life in the slave-holding South. Brown soon became bishop of the AME Church, helping spread Allen's gospel of freedom.

Meanwhile, free blacks reported an increase in discriminatory policies across the North. In New York, the new state constitution of 1821 restricted black voting rights by requiring African Americans to own $250 worth of property. In Ohio, black codes prevented African Americans from voting, serving on juries, and attending public schools.

Alarmed black leaders organized the first-ever national convention of African American reformers in September 1830. Originally the idea of a young Baltimore activist named Hezekiah Grice, the black convention movement took shape after Allen volunteered to host the inaugural meeting in Philadelphia. The first of five consecutive conventions, it took the remarkable step of considering emigration as a viable option for oppressed blacks—a measure of the anger among African Americans.

Black insurgency buoyed activist spirits. In 1831, twin slave rebellions rocked Atlantic society, showing that captive people refused to wait patiently for emancipation. The first came in August, when Nat Turner led a rebellion in Southampton County, Virginia, that lasted several days and killed more than fifty whites (including women and children) before being quashed. Turner's revolt raised alarm bells across the South. After Turner was captured and convicted, he did something remarkable for a slave rebel: he spoke. His narrative, dictated to a white lawyer and couched in the prophetic language of the Old Testament, offered a bold defense of black uprising as divinely inspired. Turner's revolt prompted the Virginia legislature to consider a gradual abolition plan for the first time in years. While it never passed, the debate proved that slave rebellion could get masters' attention.

Soon after Turner's death, a massive slave rebellion shook British Jamaica. Led by a brilliant Afro-Baptist preacher named Samuel Sharp, who planned a work stoppage after Christmas, the revolt built on recent parliamentary debates over slavery's deadly nature in the Caribbean. Though colonial officials moved swiftly against Sharp, enslaved people attacked hundreds of plantations. It took two weeks for British troops to quell the uprising. Hundreds of enslaved people were executed, including Sharp. "I would rather die upon yonder gallows," he said bravely, "than live in slavery." Like the Virginia legislature, Parliament considered imperial emancipation as a way to deal with black uprising. Across the Atlantic world, even masters realized that times had changed.

Immediate abolition

In fact, the very concept of time changed. In a world where transportation innovations (canals and railroads) and improved communications (including faster presses) had shortened distances and made it possible to get information more quickly, abolitionists saw gradual abolition as passé. A new generation of Anglo-American reformers now supported immediate emancipation.

An Englishwoman already promoted such a plan. In 1824, Elizabeth Heyrick, a fearless Quaker convert, published "Immediate, Not Gradual, Abolition" in London. Deriding claims by masters that bondsmen and women were well off, she argued that slaves had a "right" to their freedom at once—"a right which it is a crime to withhold." When masters called for compensation, she responded that only enslaved people deserved recompense for their unrewarded toil. When old-line abolitionists rejected immediatism as dangerous, she and other women redoubled their commitment to it.

Heyrick and other women had already demonstrated their power in the Free Produce movement, which agitated against the use of slave-derived goods in England. By convincing grocers in Brighton, Leicester, Nottingham, and elsewhere to support their cause, women showed non-slaveholders that economic boycotts could undercut colonial slavery. Now Heyrick wanted abolitionists to back immediatism. After Wilberforce and other gradualists resisted, fearing that it would alienate Parliament, women threatened to remove their financial support from the British Anti-Slavery Society, which had been struggling since its founding in 1823. As Heyrick's views ascended, gradualism languished. Abolitionists in America circulated her pamphlet and began listening to other advocates of immediatism, including David Walker.

By the early 1830s, American abolitionists embraced immediatism too. In 1831, former gradualist William Lloyd Garrison began publishing *The Liberator* in Boston, which became the standard bearer of immediate emancipation. "I will be harsh as justice and simple as truth," he proclaimed in his opening editorial. "And I will be heard!" Both the New England Anti-Slavery Society, founded in 1832, and the American Anti-Slavery Society, created in 1833, backed immediatism as well. By the end of the decade, nearly two thousand antislavery societies calling for immediate abolition appeared from Maine to Michigan.

Immediatist antislavery societies—so called because they opposed the very idea of slavery as unethical—were filled with crusading activists who truly believed they could change the world through a soul-cleansing confrontation with slavery. Inspired by evangelical religion, which underscored the importance of conversion experiences in saving one's soul, immediate abolitionists engaged in a campaign of moral suasion aimed at converting Americans en masse to their cause. By convincing slaveholders and their allies to renounce the sin of bondage, as one reformer confidently predicted, abolitionists would liberate 1.5 million enslaved people in just a few years. Where gradualists often appeased masters and shrunk from displaying slavery's evil nature, immediate abolitionists would show *American Slavery as It Is*, as a famous book put it. And that would doom bondage in the American mind.

Published by the American Anti-Slavery Society in 1839, *American Slavery as It Is* collected information on slavery's "atrocities," from brutal punishments to horrendous daily living conditions. Based on the "testimony of a thousand witnesses," the book examined taboo topics such as "slave breeding"—the forced impregnation of enslaved women to produce child property—as well as the discomfiting subject of "assaults, maimings," and "murders" in bondage. "Reader," the introduction asked, "what have you to say of such treatment? Is it right, just, benevolent? Suppose I should seize you, rob you of your liberty, drive you into the field, and make you work without pay as long as you live, would that be justice and kindness, or monstrous injustice and cruelty?" The lengthy list of shocking stories was designed to force Americans to confront, and ultimately reject, slavery.

Abolitionist books like this, and the moral suasion campaigns behind them, were unthinkable without the Second Great Awakening. Envisioning humans as moral free agents, nineteenth-century revivalists argued that Americans had the ability to decide their eternal fate by accepting or rejecting sin. According to Charles Grandison Finney, whose dynamic revivals in New York, New England, and Ohio mobilized waves of followers, "good works"—not predestined fates—reflected one's choice, putting people on a path to salvation. Finney's followers made their commitment to righteousness visible in a host of reform struggles. Temperance advocates railed against the excesses of alcohol consumption. Domestic missionaries promoted Bible societies and Sunday schools. And social reformers opposed prostitution, gambling, and bawdy forms of entertainment. In the revivalist mind, nothing was preordained, and all sins could be solved by conversion and good works. During the 1830s, revivalists saw abolitionism as the next great moral crusade of saints against sinners.

Yet immediate abolitionists also saw slavery as a violation of human rights. According to the American Anti-Slavery Society's founding charter, "The Declaration of Sentiments," slavery was a "crime": "No man has a right to enslave or imbrute his brother—to hold or acknowledge him, for one moment, as a piece of merchandise." Citing the Declaration of Independence, it noted that the human "right to enjoy liberty is inalienable" and that "every man has a right to his own body—to the products of his own labor—to the protection of law—and to the common advantages of society." Slavery violated a panoply of rights: the right to control one's body, to think freely, to earn a just wage, to be free from violence at the hands of individuals or governments, and to have access to legal protections. With these moral and ethical violations in mind, immediate abolitionists declared that "the slaves ought instantly to be set free, and brought under the protection of law."

Despite such clear convictions, abolitionists could not always agree on how immediate emancipation should occur. Some reformers supported government buyouts of bondage while others insisted that masters must liberate enslaved people without compensation. Some abolitionists believed that former slaves should immediately enjoy voting rights, while others envisioned a transition period for bondspeople. Some abolitionists sanctioned slave uprisings while others believed in pacifism. More than a singular doctrine, immediatism was a broad ideological standard with many variations.

The British government established a towering abolitionist standard when Parliament passed a colonial emancipation law. Taking effect on August 1, 1834, it liberated roughly seven hundred thousand enslaved people in twenty-four different British colonies. It also paid 20 million pounds to British masters and created an apprenticeship program that required liberated slaves to work as indentured laborers for six years. After black and white abolitionists campaigned against it, Parliament ended the apprentice system on August 1, 1838.

The act of emancipation propelled Great Britain to global abolitionist leadership. Across the Atlantic world, abolitionists celebrated August 1 as an emancipation day. From Boston to Baltimore and Toronto to Trinidad, reformers held rallies, gave speeches, and participated in marches that hailed Great Britain as a liberator and condemned slaveholding nations (especially the United States) as retrograde.

Although Americans celebrated British emancipation, many abolitionists opposed compensation. "If compensation is to be given at all," the American Anti-Slavery Society declared, "it should be given to the outraged and guiltless slaves, and not to those who have plundered and abused them." Falling back on moral suasion, the AASS sought to convince governments and slaveholders alike to embrace immediate emancipation.

Despite its seeming naiveté, moral suasion had a coercive side that made it hard to ignore. Working through civic and religious institutions, American abolitionists sought to pressure slaveholders and limit their legal and political options within the United States. For instance, by channeling popular anger against slaveholders into coherent government policies, including emancipation in Washington, DC, and even a constitutional amendment banning bondage throughout the nation, abolitionists believed they could essentially strangle slavery.

It all began with grassroots mobilization. Amos Phelps, a Massachusetts clergyman who converted to immediate abolition soon after joining the ACS, advocated spreading abolitionist "sentiment" through churches, schools, and families. At each step, Phelps encouraged people "to think about the slave" and abolition's power to compel moral change. From there, abolitionists would join together in immediate abolition societies and agitate against both slavery and racial injustice.

Phelps would not be disappointed in abolitionists' grassroots organizing campaigns. During the 1830s, they embarked on a massive outreach campaign that spread immediate abolition into American cities, towns, and villages. Forming female antislavery societies, young men's antislavery societies, even juvenile antislavery societies, grassroots abolitionists vowed to confront American bondage in society, law, and politics.

The American Anti-Slavery Society diffused moral suasion principles via an agency system that sent lecturers across the country. Working with local activists in Worcester, Rochester, Pittsburgh, Cincinnati, and myriad other locales, traveling lecturers formed a powerful social network of like-minded reformers. Unlike previous generations of activists, immediate abolitionists worked full time in the movement. Lecturers, organizers, and publicists pledged their very lives to the cause. It was exhausting but exhilarating work.

Perhaps the greatest antislavery agent was a revivalist who spread abolition in the West: Theodore Dwight Weld. The son of a Connecticut minister, Weld converted to immediate abolitionism after meeting Arthur Tappan and Lewis Tappan in New York City. The Tappans had recently converted to immediatism after meeting Finney. They backed William Lloyd Garrison and then co-sponsored the American Anti-Slavery Society, which held its founding meeting in Philadelphia but was based in New York. Turning to Weld, they committed to building abolitionist constituencies across the land.

Though he would become famous as the author of *American Slavery as It Is*, Weld achieved his first success as an abolitionist agent at Lane Theological Seminary in Ohio. While Lane was supposed to train the next generation of frontier ministers, its Cincinnati location (across the river from slaveholding Kentucky) made the school ripe for debates over slavery. With this in mind, Weld mobilized an extended campus discussion of emancipation in February 1834. For eighteen straight days, students debated two main topics: Should southern masters embrace immediate abolition? And did the colonization movement deserve the support of a "Christian public"? The Lane student body was composed of slaveholding sons, advocates of colonization, and even free blacks, making each night of debate intense. James Thome, who hailed from Kentucky slaveholders, agreed with Weld that bondage was brutal and became an abolitionist. James Bradley, who purchased his freedom from bondage, offered the most moving testimony. "I do not believe that there ever was a slave who did not long for liberty," he observed.

The Lane debates ended with the creation of a student antislavery society. Threatened with expulsion by the administration, the rebels issued a scathing public rebuke of Lane's leaders. Newspapers around the country reported on the fiery campus debates, including *The Liberator*. Ultimately, seventy-five students departed Lane—most of the student body. Many of these "Lane rebels" went to Oberlin College, which became a hotbed of reform.

For Weld, the Lane debate proved that moral suasion worked. Soon after, he gathered a group of abolitionist lecturers in New York City known as "The Seventy." Sending them across America to replicate the Lane experience, he hoped to build a mass movement from the ground up.

Core abolitionists: African Americans and women

In a democratizing age, no reform movement, political party, or learned institution was more diverse than abolitionism. For instance, many abolitionists were outraged by Indian removal in the late 1830s, and they chastised state and federal governments for trampling on Native people's rights during the antebellum era. John Beeson, a British abolitionist who settled in the United

States, became a longtime critic of Native mistreatment. He saw the struggle for black and Native justice as interconnected, for, as later put it, the "oppression of both races [was] united in the 'sum of all villainies.'" When he published *A Plea for the Indian*, Garrison encouraged his readers to "buy the work."

Within the growing antislavery movement, African Americans and women played critical roles during the 1820s and 1830s. In England, antislavery women transformed the abolitionist struggle while in the United States both African Americans and women became core activists of a newly aggressive abolitionism. Indeed, because they were marginalized from formal electoral politics, both black and female reformers felt unconstrained by the norms guiding Anglo-American political culture, giving abolition itself a more confrontational edge and outlook.

This was especially important on the racial justice front. In the United States, immediate abolitionists attacked northern racism as well as southern slavery. In Ohio, dozens of students pressed Lane Seminary officials to admit African Americans, while in Connecticut black and white abolitionists rallied around Prudence Crandall's attempt to integrate her own school. A Quaker teacher, Crandall initially ran afoul of Connecticut officials when she admitted a young black student to her well-regarded academy in Canterbury. Working with abolitionists, she then opened a boarding school for African American women, prompting the state legislature to take the remarkable step of banning such institutions without local approval. Crandall eventually closed her school and moved to the Midwest. Her efforts did leave an impression, however, as local abolitionists helped repeal the so-called black law in the late 1830s. "Connecticut [is] coming around," the *Colored American* newspaper declared.

Here and elsewhere, black and white reformers worked together to usher in a new era of interracial abolitionism. Vowing to fight prejudice in society, they crossed the color line by forming integrated abolition societies. While blacks had always been a part of the antislavery struggle, they rarely joined formal abolitionist organizations. The Pennsylvania Abolition Society did not admit black members until the 1840s. Yet when the New England Anti-Slavery Society formed in 1832, one quarter of its members were black. Similarly, both the Boston and the Philadelphia Female Antislavery Societies were co-founded by interracial cadres of leaders. Immediate antislavery societies in New York, Ohio, Michigan, and other states followed suit.

William Lloyd Garrison's career was deeply indebted to black activism. As a young editor at the *Genius of Universal Emancipation*, he first encountered David Walker's uncompromising *Appeal*, which inspired Garrison to become more militant. At *The Liberator,* Garrison adopted Walker's confrontational style, using exclamation points and crusading editorials to condemn both slavery and racism. In many ways, Garrison was the first "Elvis Presley" figure in American culture. By adopting an identifiably black style, Garrison gained notoriety and fame. Some longtime black activists saw Garrison as a pale imitation of Walker; others saw him as a powerful mediator who diffused black ideas throughout mainstream culture.

The deeper truth is that Garrison never shied away from his reliance on black activists, including Boston's James Barbadoes and Philadelphia's James Forten, both of whom counseled the young printer on immediatism and anti-colonization struggles. Garrison also printed black voices. During its early years, roughly one-fifth of *The Liberator*'s intellectual content came from African Americans. Little wonder that free blacks comprised more than three-quarters of the paper's initial subscribers.

Like others, Garrison also realized that women were a rising force in abolitionist circles. While at *The Genius*, he worked alongside Elizabeth Margaret Chandler, a talented writer who challenged women to become a vanguard of immediate abolition. A Quaker reformer attuned to international affairs, Chandler was inspired by British women's activism. Reading his colleague's editorials, Garrison saw women as another key constituency of immediate abolitionism.

Throughout the 1830s, a steady stream of female activists joined the abolitionist crusade: Angelina Grimké, Sarah Grimké, Lydia Maria Child, Maria Stewart, and Sojourner Truth. Serving as editors, writers, and grassroots organizers, American women brought abolitionism into homes, schools, and other institutions. In doing so, they forced even the most radical abolitionists to think about gender relations. In Philadelphia, Lucretia Mott became one of the most important abolitionists during the 1820s for her support of the Free Produce Movement—yet she was not invited to be a delegate to the American Anti-Slavery Society's founding convention in December 1833. Mott came anyway and spoke up about the power and importance of immediatism. She made an indelible impression and was soon viewed as a movement leader.

Something similar happened in small towns across the North. In case after case, women became lead activists, planning petition drives to state and federal governments and mobilizing friends and family to support the abolitionist cause. In one Massachusetts town, women outvoted men to form an antislavery society—a remarkable thing considering they could not vote in formal political elections. That they did so spoke volumes about women's impact on abolitionism and abolitionism's impact on social reform.

The grind: antislavery work

Whether men or women, black or white, American abolitionists faced daunting prospects. The experiences of South Carolina sisters Angelina and Sarah Grimké illuminate the grueling and dangerous work abolitionists did. Hailing from slave country, they witnessed the brutalizing treatment of enslaved people. Sarah questioned bondage on her father's plantation after seeing an enslaved woman violently reprimanded. After she moved to Philadelphia and joined a Quaker meeting, Angelina followed. They eventually moved to Providence, Rhode Island, and joined the American Anti-Slavery Society.

After meeting Theodore Dwight Weld—who would soon marry Angelina—the Grimké sisters went on a lecture tour that included sixty stops. Like others immediate abolitionists, they condemned slavery in harsh tones. As Angelina Grimké put it in 1837, "We affirm that *every slaveholder is a man stealer*" and "that the North is guilty of the crime of slaveholding" too for not stopping the "*national* sin" of bondage. Sarah blasted southern clergy, proclaiming that "the [southern] church is fostering [sin] in her bosom." "What an appalling spectacle do we now present! With one hand we clasp the cross of Christ, and with the other grasp the neck of the downtrodden slave!" Hoping that ministers would lead an abolitionist crusade inside the South, Sarah claimed that immediate emancipation offered masters the only way to avert eternal damnation. Angelina asked southern women to lead the abolitionist charge. In her 1836 pamphlet, "An Appeal to the Christian Women of the South," she wrote that "this horrible system of oppression and cruelty, licentiousness and wrong" would not last if white women condemned it. "You are now loudly called upon... to arise and gird yourselves for this great moral conflict," she continued. Despite threats, the Grimké sisters soldiered on.

In Ohio, Betsy Mix Cowles matched the Grimké sisters' activism by becoming a powerhouse organizer. The daughter of a Connecticut minister who migrated to Ohio, Cowles was originally set to be a schoolteacher. Instead, she became a fearless abolitionist, helping to organize the Ashtabula Female Antislavery Society in 1835. Attracting four hundred members, the society became one of the largest abolitionist groups in Ohio. Cowles condemned Ohio's black laws as unjust, and she aided runaway slaves. Like the Grimké sisters, Cowles refused to back down from public rebukes or physical intimidation.

African Americans often faced the harshest abuse. In New England, lecturers Hosea Easton and James Barbadoes spoke before integrated audiences that their opponents labeled "amalgamationist." Worried that race-mixing threatened the American republic, anti-abolitionists insulted black speakers and physically broke up abolitionist meetings. Still, black abolitionists believed that they had a moral duty to confront race prejudice above the Mason-Dixon line. Boston's Maria Stewart challenged African Americans to become more militant agitators for racial justice. "Why sit ye here and die," she asked one audience? Stewart's work impressed Garrison, who reprinted her speeches in *The Liberator*. The first female activist to lecture before a "promiscuous audience" (of men and women), she also protested the idea that female reformers must defer to men.

Black abolitionists constantly pushed other reformers to embrace more forceful tactics. New York City's David Ruggles espoused "practical abolition," which favored hands-on resistance activities (including civil disobedience and physical self-defense). He practiced what he preached by leading the New York Vigilance Committee, a group that aided hundreds of kidnapped free blacks and runaway slaves. Ruggles roamed the city streets searching for distressed African Americans. His most famous rescue was a young man who escaped Maryland bondage in 1838: Frederick Douglass. Ruggles brought him to a safe house and facilitated his departure for Massachusetts. In Philadelphia, Detroit, and other locales, African Americans created vigilance groups that replicated Ruggles's confrontational style, making clear that abolitionism was a matter of life and death for people of color.

Bold activism

Throughout the 1830s, immediate abolitionists experimented with new tactics designed to ignite emancipation debate. From expanding the agency system in the North to publishing a host of antislavery newspapers—*The Emancipator, The Abolitionist, The Colored American, The Liberty Bell*—second-wave reformers tried every means possible to reach American hearts and minds.

In 1835, they flooded the U.S. mail system with antislavery literature destined for slaveholders themselves. In Charleston, South Carolina, slaveholders established a vigilance committee to monitor such abolitionist incursions. When the mailings appeared, alarmed residents returned them to the post office. As one Charleston newspaper reported, this "moral poison" was designed to foment slave insurrection. A mob seized and burned abolitionist mailings alongside effigies of Garrison.

Abolitionists complained that their free speech rights had been abrogated and called on the federal government to protect their mail campaigns. Alerted to the matter by Postmaster General Amos Kendall, President Andrew Jackson expressed his intense dislike of abolitionists, whom he called "monsters" intent on stirring up a "servile war" in the South. Yet Jackson conceded abolitionists' point about civil liberties, at least in theory. Jackson and Kendall thus agreed that abolitionist mailings could be delivered to southerners who "will demand them as subscribers"—a scare tactic designed to expose slavery's opponents. Local authorities even published the names of would-be abolitionist readers. Few people came forward.

When abolitionists flooded Congress with antislavery petitions, southern politicians secured the nation's first-ever gag rule. From 1836 through 1844, it stipulated that all antislavery memorials must "be laid upon the [congressional] table without being debated, printed, read or refined and that no action whatsoever shall be had there on." Undeterred, abolitionists continued to send petitions to the federal government.

Most abolitionist petitions were signed by women and young men. Yet this did not mean that abolitionist discussion was limited to these groups. Rather, women often signed abolitionist petitions after discussing the matter with family members, neighbors, church leaders, and friends. Even when they signed on their own, women claimed their First Amendment rights to examine a controversial but important matter: human freedom. A memorial from Philadelphia women "respectfully" asked Congress to consider ending slavery in the District of Columbia because "[we] believe that if our general government act to the extent of their power in removing this evil [from the District], their example may have a happy influence on the legislatures of the southern states." Indeed, while abolitionists were "aware that at this juncture our attempt may be considered intrusive," they reminded Congress that "we approach you unarmed; our only banner is peace." The petition had 2,211 signatures affixed to it, all of them by women.

The anti-abolitionist wall in the North

While abolitionists continued to agitate against slavery, they discovered that the free speech issue resonated with many northerners. They began working on dual tracks: circulating antislavery materials and raising awareness about threats to civil liberties. As abolitionists knew, southern states were not alone in policing free speech. Even in Massachusetts, state officials debated whether to suppress abolitionism. From books to newspaper editorials, abolitionists responded by defending their right to speak and publish on divisive social issues like slavery.

Such bravado did not prevent attacks on abolitionists. In fact, a wave of anti-abolitionist riots occurred during the 1830s, sending a collective shudder through the movement. Rioters attacked

THE ABOLITION GARRISON IN DANGER, & THE NARROW
ESCAPE of the SCOTCH AMBASSADOR.

Boston Oct. 21st 1835.

5. Abolitionists faced mobs across the North during the 1830s. Garrison was dragged through the streets of Boston while one of his fellow speakers, British abolitionist George Thompson (labeled here as the Scotch Ambassador) received several death threats. Unsympathetic artists parodied abolitionists' perilous struggles.

reformers in Boston, New York City, and Utica, among other locales. They included both upper-class whites, whose economic ties to the South made abolitionism a financial threat, and members of the working class, who opposed racial equality in the job market. Rioters often targeted the most visible reformers. Garrison was dragged through the streets of Boston while Ruggles was constantly harassed. Mobs attacked reformers who upset social norms, ranging from interracial gatherings to events featuring women and men on the same public platform.

The worst rioting of the decade occurred in abolition's birthplace. In May 1838, a mob burned down "Pennsylvania Hall," a gleaming new edifice in the heart of Philadelphia where "liberty and equality of civil rights [should] be freely discussed," as former president John Quincy Adams put it in a letter to abolitionists. Immediately after the building was inaugurated, abolitionists staged a convention of antislavery women, which prompted

THE DISAPPOINTED ABOLITIONISTS.

6. Immediate abolitionism was an interracial cause—something that anti-abolitionists in both the North and the South condemned. This image mocks African American reformer David Ruggles (center) and his white abolitionist colleagues for engaging in race-mixing lectures and other activities.

an outcry from many white citizens. A mob gathered outside Pennsylvania Hall, threatening an interracial group of abolitionists inside. In a stirring scene, antislavery women joined arms and bravely pushed through the angry crowd. After just four days, anti-abolitionists broke into the building and started a fire. As the building went up in flames, fire companies watched. Pennsylvania Hall was never rebuilt. Worse, abolitionists were blamed as the troublemakers who incited mob action.

Mobs tried to silence the movement well beyond Philadelphia. Abolitionist editor Jane Swisshelm moved from Pittsburgh to Minnesota but found she could not escape the wrath of anti-abolition agitators even in this far northern locale. In St. Cloud, a mob destroyed her printing press during the 1850s; unfazed, she launched a new paper. In Alton, Illinois, Elijah Lovejoy paid the ultimate price for his abolitionist work. After moving his newspaper from St. Louis to escape pro-slavery mobs, he found similar opposition in Illinois, where locals upbraided him for holding antislavery meetings that threatened the region's

7. In May 1838, Pennsylvania Hall, a grand new building dedicated to abolitionism and free speech in Philadelphia, was burned to the ground by arsonists. Elsewhere, abolitionist editors were harassed, threatened, and even killed.

economic ties to the South. Lovejoy refused to stop publishing his abolitionist newspaper. When a mob tracked him down on November 7, 1837, Lovejoy battled back but he was killed defending his right to criticize slavery. The mob tossed his press into the Mississippi River. No one was convicted in Lovejoy's death.

Anti-abolitionist violence proved that many Americans saw immediate abolitionism as simply too radical, especially when it focused on racial equality. Of course, southern slaveholders opposed immediatism as a violation of their constitutional right to hold human property. They delighted in anti-abolitionist crackdowns and even called for them above the Mason-Dixon line as an act of fealty to the nation. Facing such terrible odds, it is a miracle that abolitionists did not give up the fight.

Chapter 4
The abolitionist crossroads

After the turbulent 1830s, doubt and discord haunted the antislavery ranks. Facing opposition North and South, immediate abolitionists quarreled not only with their opponents but also with each other. A series of questions loomed: Should abolitionists moderate their protest or become even more radical? Should they form a political party or separate from corrupt civil and religious institutions? Should they aid fugitive slaves or embrace nonviolence? Should women and African Americans assume roles of greater or lesser prominence in the antislavery movement?

American abolitionists were not the only reformers at a crossroads. After successfully pushing for an emancipation law, British abolitionists retooled by aiding antislavery struggles around the globe, while French abolitionists revived debates over abolition in the Caribbean. And Spanish and Portuguese reformers focused on eradicating the slave trade, which still transported thousands of African captives to the Caribbean and South America. Just like the previous decade, the 1840s were a time of dynamism and change for abolitionism.

Abolitionist divisions: From the woman question to antislavery political parties

For American abolitionists, the most divisive internal issue proved to be women's role in the movement. After working as lecturers, organizers, and editors, women demanded leadership roles in the American Anti-Slavery Society (AASS). When conservative figures—especially ministers who believed that women's activism created more opposition to abolition—pushed back, the movement fragmented.

The "woman question" had deep roots. Beyond their work at the AASS, antislavery women had already illustrated their leadership mettle by organizing a series of national conventions. In May 1837, the American Convention of Antislavery Women held its inaugural meeting in New York City, attracting nearly two hundred delegates from ten states. Two subsequent conventions followed in Philadelphia, including the ill-fated 1838 meeting at Pennsylvania Hall. Undeterred by civic opposition, women's conventions condemned Christian churches for accepting money from slaveholders, encouraged female abolitionists to identify with enslaved women in the South, and vowed to continue petition campaigns to state and federal governments. These national conventions also spawned future leaders of the women's rights movement, including Lucretia Mott and Elizabeth Cady Stanton, who planned the famed 1848 Seneca Falls Convention.

At the AASS, Abigail Kelley's appointment to the Business Committee in 1840 brought the "woman question" to a head. Kelley was a rising star whose supporters saw her as the movement's future. The daughter of a Massachusetts farm family, she converted to abolitionism after coming under the sway of antislavery Quakers in the manufacturing town of Lynn. Inspired by Garrison, she became a renowned lecturer, fundraiser, and organizer. In one congressional petition campaign, Kelley mobilized nearly half the women of Lynn.

Yet several prominent men opposed Kelley's ascension at the AASS, including Arthur Tappan, Lewis Tappan, Amos Phelps, and William Jay. After Garrison and others supported Kelley, conservatives bolted to form a rival organization, the American and Foreign Antislavery Society (AFASS). Publishing a stream of pamphlets and their own newspaper (*The American and Foreign Anti-Slavery Society Reporter*), the group argued that a big tent version of abolition was better suited to the times. Back at the AASS, Garrison filled the void with "ultra" abolitionists who backed women's rights, pacifism, and moral perfectionism.

The rise of "ultra" abolitionists indicates that other issues roiled the movement in the 1840s. Many AFASS supporters saw Garrison as ego-driven and increasingly doctrinaire on such issues as "nonresistance," or the rejection of violence. Garrison also saw party politics as inherently corrupt and famously labeled the Constitution "a covenant with death and an agreement with hell" (from Isaiah 28:18). Finally, Garrison continued to rebuke non-slaveholding Christians for tolerating bondage, a tactic that upset potential supporters. "Moderate your indignation and keep more cool," a reformer counseled Garrison, "why, you are all on fire." "I have need to be all on fire, for I have mountains of ice about me to melt," Garrison countered.

Garrison's rivals in the AFASS favored an ecumenical approach to abolitionism and embraced the formation of antislavery political parties. With the support of the Tappan brothers and Gerrit Smith, a wealthy philanthropist who joined the abolitionist crusade in the wake of mob violence near his home in Hamilton, New York, the Liberty Party took shape. It had an inauspicious debut in the election of 1840. Running former slaveholder James

Gillespie Birney as president on a platform that favored emancipation in the nation's capital and restrictions on slavery's western growth, the Liberty Party tallied a mere seven thousand votes. Four years later, the Liberty Party got sixty thousand votes.

Political abolitionists like Birney were not deterred by these paltry results. Believing that abolitionists had a political and not just a moral duty to oppose slavery, they argued that northerners tired of the temporizing policies of the Whig and Democratic Parties would soon support antislavery candidates. Fomenting outrage at the "slave power"—the proslavery band of supporters in the federal government—they provided a political alternative for northern voters. Though it experienced growing pains, the Liberty Party matured, holding national nominating conventions and launching a party periodical in 1847. Liberty candidates gained support in New England, Michigan, New York, and Ohio and began disrupting national politics. In 1844, the Liberty Party siphoned off just enough votes in New York to scuttle Whig candidate (and Kentucky slaveholder) Henry Clay's presidential bid. While another slaveholder, James Polk, took office, Liberty voters showed that they could have an impact on political results.

To keep pace with their rivals' efforts, the American Anti-Slavery Society broadened its outreach efforts. The group launched a new newspaper in 1840: *The National Antislavery Standard.* Run by Lydia Maria Child and her husband, David Child, the paper was published concurrently in Philadelphia and New York City, allowing the group to better compete with the AFASS beyond New England. Like Garrison, *The Standard* rebuked slaveholders, northern anti-abolitionists, and others for letting slavery and racial injustice grow. "The object for which we are associated is the abolition of slavery—not to build up or to pull down the clerical profession," the paper proclaimed. If ministers, politicians, and citizens felt threatened by abolitionist rebukes, they were on the wrong side of slavery.

8. Frederick Douglass was celebrated as an abolitionist hero in art, engravings, and photography. This image, which appeared in Julia Griffiths' book, *Autographs for Freedom* (New York, 1854), reveals Douglass's intense commitment to the abolitionist struggle.

To propel its message beyond the eastern seaboard, the AASS planned a massive lecture tour in 1843. Known as the One Hundred Conventions tour, it brought agents into Indiana, western New York, Ohio, and western Pennsylvania. While Garrison traveled west, his lecturing partner Frederick Douglass became the tour's big star. Indeed, after Garrison returned to

Boston with an illness, Douglass led the tour into areas where few people really understood abolition. "All the people needed was light," he argued, and they would embrace abolition. Despite his optimism in moral suasion, Douglass was mobbed in Pendleton, Indiana. Like others, he forged ahead, refusing to let a broken arm stop him from spreading abolitionist light.

Abolitionist synergies

Ironically, abolitionist divisions may have expanded the movement's scope and reach. Competing abolitionist groups constantly sought new ways of mobilizing supporters, thereby increasing the number of abolitionist publications, lecture tours, and conventions. By midcentury, there were enough varieties within the antislavery fold that reformers could find some group or personality that matched their own sense of purpose.

Distinct abolitionist paths often converged. Particularly in the Midwest, local abolition societies found ways to work with both political abolitionists and moral suasionists. More broadly, abolitionist factions often articulated similar visions of protest. Just as Garrisonians emphasized the importance of severing ties to corrupt institutions—whether churches or governments—so too did the AFASS support "come outer" congregations: reform churches that refused to align with slaveholders. Maria Weston Chapman, who helped found the Boston Female Anti-Slavery Society and remained a leading figure in the AASS, wrote passionately about separating from corrupt religious bodies. Political abolitionist James Birney essentially agreed, arguing that since "the American church is the bulwark of American slavery," congregants themselves must lead an exodus from sin. William Goodell, who aligned with Birney and opposed Garrison, went a step further, calling it a "duty" of Christians to leave proslavery churches. No matter their affiliation, abolitionists sounded awfully alike.

Their combined efforts challenged slavery anew. By 1850, "come outers" comprised nearly a quarter million Americans. Though still a minority of the faithful, "come outers" raised the stakes of abolition by establishing "free" churches. In Boston, the American and Foreign Baptist Mission Society formed after one-time slaveholder William Henry Brisbane's call for an emancipated church. Brisbane left his native South Carolina after receiving an abolitionist pamphlet that convinced him of slavery's wrong. Settling in Cincinnati, he sought like-minded Baptists before forming his own church. The result was a small but committed group of religious dissenters, which moved to Boston. As Garrison gleefully noted in *The Liberator*, the Baptist Missionary Society's new constitution asserted "that involuntary slavery, under all circumstances, is sin" and the church would not accept slaveholders. Lutherans, Wesleyans, Methodists, and others developed "free" churches too. In New York, Henry Fowler's Second Presbyterian "free" Church supported abolition while the Frankean Synod, a radical Lutheran sect, declared "it to be our imperative duty to speak boldly and plainly against this great national and heinous sin [of slavery]."

With abolitionists pressing from inside religious communities, mainline Protestant denominations found it hard to avoid the slavery issue. By midcentury, the Baptist, Methodist, and Presbyterian denominations split into northern and southern groups.

Fractious abolitionists rallied around another cause: the Amistad slave rebels. In July 1839, fifty-three Africans revolted on a small Cuban slave ship with the ironic name of *La Amistad* (friendship in Spanish). The captives had been illegally seized in West Africa by Portuguese traders and shipped to Havana, where they were purchased and transferred to a Cuban plantation. Under the leadership of a valiant man named Cinque, they took over the ship and demanded a return to Africa. Surviving crew members steered north, however, and *La Amistad* was captured by U.S. forces near Long Island. Put into a Connecticut prison, the

African contingent awaited its fate. Pressed by Spanish authorities, American political representatives, including emissaries of the proslavery Democratic president Martin Van Buren, pledged to extradite the rebels to Spanish Cuba.

Abolitionists mobilized a massive publicity campaign against Spanish rendition. Newspapers attacked efforts to reenslave the rebels while black and white abolitionists held fundraising events. The rebels' legal challenge was bankrolled by the Tappan brothers, but it drew support from Garrisonians too. In New Haven, Yale students and professors sympathetic to the abolitionist cause found translators for the African men and women huddled in the dank prison. Abolitionist unity scared slaveholders. South Carolinian John C. Calhoun did not worry about abolitionist divisions; rather, he focused his criticism on *Amistad* activism, which he decried as yet another northern attempt to interfere with slaveholders' rights. The case eventually came to the Supreme Court, where the Tappan brothers prevailed upon former president John Quincy Adams to argue on the rebels' behalf. In 1841, the Supreme Court liberated the rebels. Sadly, only thirty-five *Amistad* rebels were still alive. But they were returned to West Africa.

Global abolitionism in the 1840s

On the international scene, the 1840s saw a renewed spirit of abolitionist mobilization. Buoyed by the success of the Emancipation Act, British abolitionists organized the inaugural World Antislavery Convention in London, which gathered reformers from Great Britain, the European continent, and the United States. Despite its attempt to build consensus, the convention could not escape debates roiling the U.S. movement. When it convened in June 1840, the convention's organizers would not seat women, including luminaries like Lucretia Mott and Elizabeth Cady Stanton. Mott challenged British officials but to no avail. When a Jamaican delegate said that women's participation would devalue the meeting, she replied that the same thing had been said about admitting African Americans to U.S. abolition societies. Women were eventually seated as "guests" but Mott and Stanton vowed to push more fervently for women's rights in America.

The contretemps notwithstanding, the World Antislavery Convention was a success. Nearly five hundred delegates examined a range of important issues, from slavery's spread in the southwestern United States to the continuing problem of the overseas slave trade to Russian serfdom. Perhaps two thousand people watched the proceedings, with no riots or violent outbursts occurring.

The convention solidified British leadership in transatlantic abolitionism. In 1838, reformers founded the British and Foreign Anti-Slavery Society (BFASS) to spur "universal emancipation" overseas. Though ostensibly focused on freedom in the British Empire, the BFASS's constitution sought to protect "all persons captured as slaves" and stop the "sale and barter of human beings." The group met annually, corresponded with abolitionists throughout Atlantic society, and relaunched *The Antislavery Reporter* to draw attention to emancipation debates in France, slave-trading Brazil, and concerns over unfree labor in British India.

Led by a combination of rising and established reformers—from George Thompson, who came on the scene in the 1830s, to longtime Quaker activist William Allen—British abolitionists helped Americans sharpen their defense of immediate abolition. Where critics blasted immediate emancipation as chaotic, British abolitionists hailed it as successful. Indeed, the lesson of British emancipation in the Caribbean was that it should have occurred sooner and without the terrible obstacle of apprenticeship for former slaves. Thompson spread this message on lecture tours of the United States, where he often faced hostile crowds. Thompson called emancipation safe and told audiences from New York to New England that the facts of freedom were on his side. Even after fleeing the "assassin's knife," and returning to

The abolitionist crossroads

England, Thompson's reprinted lectures on slavery and abolition galvanized American reformers.

Joseph Sturge picked up where Thompson left, touring the United States in the 1840s with positive reports about British emancipation. By then, Sturge was already known for his influential fact-finding mission on the horrors of apprenticeship in the Caribbean. Sturge's pamphlet on the matter convinced Parliament to convert apprenticeship into total emancipation in 1838. From then on, Sturge made clear, free labor systems were working well. Indeed, by midcentury, productivity and exports in many colonies had returned to pre-emancipation levels.

British defenses of emancipation came at a critical time. Building on years of anti-abolitionist thinking, a new generation of American masters and their allies created the "positive good" thesis about slavery. From Jamaica to the U.S. North, they claimed, emancipation had failed, justifying slavery anew. Far from a lunatic fringe, emancipation's critics included doctors, scientists, and professors at northern as well as southern institutions. Samuel George Morton, who taught at the University of Pennsylvania medical school, launched the so-called American School of Ethnography, which espoused polygenesis, or the theory of separate races. Cataloguing people according to skull and brain sizes, Morton established a hierarchy of racial types, with "white" (Euro-American) groups at the top and "black" (non-Western) people below. Samuel Cartwright and Josiah Nott, well-known physicians who trained at northern medical schools, eagerly adopted ethnological models of black inferiority. Cartwright depicted runaway slaves as delusional maniacs who suffered from "Drapetomania," a sickness that compelled them to escape benign bondage. New Yorker Dr. John Van Evrie, perhaps the most prolific proslavery writer in the North, called global emancipation folly and abolitionists insane.

Abolitionists pushed back by celebrating emancipation's successes. American reformers produced studies showing that African

Americans were just as industrious as whites in northern cities (W. E. B. DuBois's *The Philadelphia Negro* was modeled on abolitionist censuses). They also toured free black settlements in British Canada and the Caribbean to show that emancipation worked. After traveling to Antigua, Barbados, and Jamaica, former Lane Rebel James Thome reported that there was "no danger in the immediate emancipation of the negro." Labeling liberty a "right" for people of color no less than whites, he called former slaves everywhere "fit for...freedom."

Given these debates over emancipation's future, abolitionists celebrated when France (under a new republican government) passed a universal emancipation law in 1848. Though pushed by a relatively small band of Parisian abolitionists, it was framed by years of black agitation. For years, free people of color had challenged political disfranchisement while enslaved people protested against the reestablishment of bondage in places such as Guadeloupe and Martinique. In fact, the threat of slave rebellion compelled the French government to implement compensated abolition plans faster than initially planned.

Unlike Anglo-American abolition, the French antislavery struggle was not defined by mass action or sweeping evangelical beliefs. While supporters included such luminaries as Victor Hugo and Alexis de Tocqueville, French petition campaigns were relatively modest. Led by competent government officials like Victor Schoelcher, emancipationists sought to fulfill the promises of the Revolution of 1789 by destroying slavery once and for all. They did more than that. By midcentury, French abolition made the United States even more of a global outlier.

Racial divisions in transatlantic abolition

Despite significant strides, global abolitionists could not surmount racial discord. For instance, in the British Caribbean, emancipated people registered concerns about the civilizing mission attached to abolition. Emphasizing Christian uplift principles (piety, sobriety, thrift), white abolitionists often lectured people of color about becoming good British subjects—not self-determined communities who might reject Western belief systems. Even the British navy's African Squadron, which patrolled Atlantic waters in search of slave-trading scofflaws and liberated tens of thousands of captive Africans, found itself in a conundrum: where should liberated people be sent? Emancipated blacks often found themselves in British colonies like Trinidad, where they encountered uplift ideology if not outright racism. While many liberated Africans wanted to return to their homeland, British officials believed they would be better served in post-emancipation colonies that had a civilizing mission and could prove the efficacy of abolitionism.

Similarly, Victor Schoelcher's tour of Haiti in the early 1840s exposed the gap between abolitionist ideology and the needs of free black communities. Though critical of Haitian leaders for not investing in schools and other uplift institutions, the French abolitionist focused on the country's rural population, which did not embrace free labor ideology or economic modernization. This was a "bitter and disappointing" result for the revolution in Saint-Domingue, he wrote. As historian Laurent Dubois observes, these comments illustrate how "even a leading abolitionist like Schoelcher was essentially blind to the antislavery revolution that was still underway in Haiti." For many Haitians prized autonomy and self-sufficiency over Western ideology and economic modernization.

In the United States, African Americans expressed increasing frustration with the paternalism of white abolitionists. Some whites fell into a romantic racialism that pictured enslaved people as suffering saints unprepared for the realities of freedom. Using language that reified racial hierarchies, they often objectified black people. White abolitionists also relegated free blacks to secondary roles in the movement, straining interracial alliances. Henry Highland Garnet would famously proclaim that white reformers were "our allies," not blacks' rulers, for "ours is the battle." James McCune Smith noted that black liberation would come only when African Americans freed themselves from the paternal influences of well-meaning white reformers. Sojourner Truth wondered aloud at white people's inability to see her freedom claims. "I have heard much about the sexes being equal," she commented at a women's rights convention in Akron in 1851, though few people stopped to consider her views. "I have as much muscle as any man and can do as much as any man," she continued. "I am a woman's rights." But did white women—even abolitionists—see her as equal?

African American concerns resulted in the revival of the black convention movement, which had stopped after 1835. Arguing that they needed an autonomous forum to prosecute the struggle for racial justice, blacks held nineteen state and national conventions during the 1840s. Led by a younger generation of reformers, many of whom were fugitive slaves, black conventions debated several issues, from launching a new national newspaper to backing slave revolts in the South. At the Buffalo convention of 1843, the first in eight years, Henry Highland Garnet asked free blacks to publicly sanction a slave uprising. Speaking directly to southern slaves, he proclaimed: "Brethren, arise, arise! Strike for your lives and liberties!" A fugitive slave from Maryland, Garnet believed that slavery's growth justified such pitched responses from black abolitionists. Ironically, Frederick Douglass, who would soon write about physically challenging a slave breaker in Maryland bondage, opposed Garnet's call as both impractical (because enslaved people could not overwhelm southern masters) and impolitic (because it eschewed moral suasion). After debating the matter, the convention agreed with Douglass and refused to print Garnet's proclamation. He published it anyway, along with a biography of David Walker, his hero.

Garnet's confrontational style spoke to an insurgent sensibility coursing through black communities. Traveling in New York and New England, where he campaigned for equal voting rights,

Garnet met angry black activists frustrated by the limits of moral suasion. In Detroit, black abolitionists George DeBaptiste and William Lambert did more than express their frustration—they launched the Colored Vigilance Committee, which helped roughly 1,500 fugitive slaves gain freedom (most in British Canada).

White radicals and confrontational abolitionism

Some white abolitionists responded to blacks' concerns by taking increasingly radical stands themselves. Charles Torrey, a Massachusetts abolitionist who grew weary of Garrisonian nonviolence, began risking his life to aid black runaways. With funding from Gerrit Smith, Torrey ran a clandestine escape network stretching from Washington, DC, to Albany, New York. Armed and girded for a fight, he evaded arrest until 1844, when he was captured in Maryland and sent to prison. Emaciated and unrepentant, he died after two years. But his example lived on.

Indeed, Gerrit Smith continued to support slave escapes, including an ill-fated plot to liberate nearly eighty people from Washington, DC. Organized by an interracial group that included New York abolitionist William Chaplin and former slave Paul Jennings, the daring escape took place on April 15, 1848. After the large group of runaways boarded *The Pearl* in hopes of reaching New Jersey, the ship hit unfavorable weather and was soon caught. Daniel Drayton, the abolitionist ship captain, spent years in prison while most of the recaptured slaves were sold to the Deep South.

As the *Pearl* case illustrated, one strain of the abolitionist movement believed strongly in attacking bondage from inside slave country. Part of a borderland strategy that attacked slavery's edges, abolitionists hoped to create emancipation outposts that chipped away at slavery. Border states had a relatively small percentage of enslaved people—perhaps 10 to 20 percent—and they tolerated small bands of abolitionists—as long as they did not agitate too much. Periodically, border states debated the merits of emancipation. Both Tennessee in the 1830s and Kentucky in the 1850s considered but did not pass gradual abolition schemes.

Some white abolitionists operated inside the South. Kentuckian John Fee criticized his slaveholding father as a sinner and called bondage a moral stain on the South. Identifying with his mother's Quaker roots, he studied at Lane Seminary before returning to Kentucky as a preacher and abolitionist. The Presbyterian Church asked Fee to leave the pulpit, but he refused. Dr. Gamaliel Bailey moved from Ohio, where he edited the antislavery periodical *The Philanthropist*, to Washington, DC, where he took control of another abolitionist newspaper, *The National Era*. A supporter of political abolitionism, Bailey faced consistent attacks from slavery's defenders, though, like Fee, he refused to back down.

Others left slave country but remained active on the antislavery borderland. John Rankin first promulgated abolition in his native Tennessee, and then in his adopted home of Kentucky before opposition scared him away. Settling in Cincinnati, Rankin aided hundreds of runaway slaves between the 1820s and 1850s. Virginian Moncur Conway believed that slavery violated both scripture and Jefferson's Declaration of Independence, but he ultimately departed the Old Dominion in despair. After attending school in Pennsylvania and becoming a Methodist minister, he accepted an offer to lead a Washington, DC, church. The offer disappeared when Conway's new congregation discovered his abolitionist views. He eventually settled in Cincinnati.

The Underground Railroad

Border states also had more lenient attitudes toward free blacks and allowed hired-out slaves more mobility than in the Deep South. African Americans exploited these openings to work, save money, and purchase both themselves and family members out of bondage. In Nashville, an enslaved woman named Sally Thomas was a stealth abolitionist who did what thousands of bondsmen and women did: she bargained for freedom or semi-freedom from her master. Working as a laundress, Thomas gave part of her wages to her master and secured a freedom agreement for one of her sons.

Thomas had another son who escaped north to freedom on what became known as the Underground Railroad (UGRR). Though it funneled a relatively small percentage of enslaved people to freedom—perhaps thirty thousand to sixty thousand people by 1860—the very existence of the UGRR intensified sectional debates over slavery. Indeed, the UGRR symbolized both the restiveness of blacks in bondage and the increasing willingness of white northerners to aid (or at least sympathize with) runaways, something that truly antagonized slaveholders.

Less a singular institution and more a series of interconnected networks, the UGRR had many movement centers: Detroit, Washington, DC, Philadelphia, Buffalo, Cincinnati. It also had a variety of routes. While the Mississippi and Ohio rivers funneled people north from interior regions of the border South to Cleveland, Detroit, Buffalo, and even Chicago, railroads, overland trails and ships brought freedom seekers to liberty via Atlantic seaboard cities such as Philadelphia, New York, and Boston. In the Southwest, some runaways made it to Mexico or ran into Indian country (in either territorial Florida or the trans-Mississippi West). Wherever they went, enslaved people and their allies used an elaborate system of songs and symbols, secret communications, and bold movements to move people from slavery to freedom. John Rankin left small boats along the banks of the Ohio River, and candles on poles near safe houses, to communicate with enslaved people desperately trying to outwit slave catchers. In Rochester, New York, Frederick Douglass had couriers who informed him about freedom seekers coming into the region.

While the stories of escaped slaves would rivet northern white audiences, enslaved peoples' search for liberty often began with small steps into the unknown. Henry Bibb, who fled Kentucky via an Ohio River steamboat that took him through Indiana and then to Cincinnati, shielded himself from capture before finding black allies. He then discovered "abolitionists" who helped him get to British Canada and freedom. "This was the first time in my life that I ever heard of such people," he later wrote. "I supposed they were a different race of people" altogether for their commitment to "suffering humanity." In Richmond, Virginia, Henry "Box" Brown used black and white allies to literally mail himself to freedom. Devastated by the sale of his wife and children—who were marched by him in a slave coffle—Brown vowed to get free. After sealing himself in a small box, a white dissident had Brown mailed from Richmond to Philadelphia. When he arrived, abolitionists opened the box and marveled that the delirious Brown had survived the twenty-seven-hour journey to freedom. Brown told his tale to audiences stretching from the U.S. North to England.

As Bibb and Brown's experiences illustrate, the Underground Railroad had a tangible existence—it was not just a metaphor. Networks may have been loosely formed—but there were clandestine escape networks in the North and South. Perhaps more importantly, the UGRR produced the single most effective publicity tool of the abolitionist movement: slave narratives. Although black stories of injustice had informed abolitionism since the 1700s, a host of slave narratives remade the cause during the 1840s and 1850s. Douglass's 1845 autobiography became a bestseller, inspiring many other black abolitionists to introduce themselves to Anglo-American audiences through slave narratives: William Wells Brown, Henry Box Brown, Henry Bibb, J. W. C. Pennington, William Craft and Ellen Craft, Harriet Jacobs, and many others. "This fugitive slave literature is destined to be a powerful lever" of reform, one abolitionist observed in 1849. It goes "right to the hearts" of men and women.

Slave narratives uncovered the harsh realities of bondage for mainstream American readers, who often took for granted masters' claims about bondage. Like characters in a morality play, escaped slaves navigated an evil world beset by treacherous people. Slave narratives also drew on adventure tales, taking readers on seemingly fantastic journeys from slavery to freedom. These tales entertained, saddened, shocked, and inspired American audiences—making them hate slavery more intensely than ever and challenging white readers to sympathize with African American characters.

The ever-decreasing cost of producing books and pamphlets abetted the rise of slave narratives. Abolitionist networks established by traveling lecturers and antislavery newspapers further facilitated their sale and distribution. Yet the slave narrative genre also echoed key intellectual and philosophical trends in Anglo-American culture. Tales of runaway slaves offered a dramatic counterpart to Transcendental philosophy, which valorized sacred self-sovereignty: the struggle to liberate oneself from the shackles of oppressive family, societal, and cultural institutions. Similarly, slave narratives channeled transatlantic romantic sensibilities, appealing directly to readers' emotions.

Indeed, slave narratives described bondage in the most personal terms: what it was like to see family members sold away, what harsh and cruel punishments felt like, how working all day and into the night sapped the body and soul. In doing this, slave narrators established their common humanity with white readers. In one of many heart-rending scenes in his narrative, Bibb recalled the burning heartache of standing before his family knowing he may never see them again after he escaped.

Of course, slave narrators often ended their harrowing tales in the seemingly free North. Because white abolitionists served as compilers, editors, and publishers of many slave narratives, they often accented the glories of northern freedom and abolitionism while underplaying racism above the Mason-Dixon line. Moreover, they pictured African Americans as deeply committed

Christians who needed white allies to escape the torment of bondage. Though the overwhelming majority of fugitive slave stories were true and verified, the genre was not without complications.

Yet the very act of writing a slave narrative allowed black authors to confront American hypocrisy. For slave narratives charged that white northern apathy supported bondage just as much as white southern mastery. Slave narrators literally broke through the illusion separating reader and writer to make this point. In a startling passage from his first autobiography, Henry Box Brown recalled his enslaved mother trying to protect him from slavery's innate despotism. He moved from remembrance to a real-time confrontation with the reader: "Mothers of the North! as you gaze upon the fair forms of your idolized little ones, just pause for a moment; how would you feel if you knew that at any time the will of a tyrant—who neither could nor would sympathise with your domestic feelings—might separate them for ever from your embrace…?" Brown sought to shake readers' complacency and make them into abolitionists.

No slave narrator was more important than Frederick Douglass. Soon after settling in Massachusetts, he began reading *The Liberator* and attending antislavery meetings. Urged to tell his story at an antislavery meeting, Douglass stole the show. Hearing Douglass, Garrison said that he never hated slavery so much. After piecing together parts of an autobiography on the lecture circuit, he published his narrative in 1845. Distributed under the aegis of Garrison, it became a bestseller. Douglass's autobiography told the haunting tale of a young American full of promise who was nearly lost to slavery. He never knew his father (likely a white overseer on a Maryland plantation) and barely knew his mother. Even as a boy, Douglass learned the harsh lessons of bondage: enslaved people were deemed property and they had no rights whatsoever—not even the right to learn the alphabet. Despite the odds, Douglass fought back literally and figuratively by learning to read, vanquishing his white overseer, and eventually escaping to the North. Douglass was the classic American underdog, and his story was perfectly pitched to a democratic citizenry proud of its revolutionary stands against oppressive authority.

In Massachusetts, Douglass initially hoped to melt into the free black community. But he felt compelled to join the abolitionist crusade. When he wrote his autobiography, Douglass challenged white readers to go and do likewise.

The North Star international

Douglass's celebrity forced him to flee America, lest his master recapture the most famous fugitive in the land. After successful lecture tours in Great Britain, he thought about remaining overseas, where racism appeared less virulent. Yet Douglass also felt strongly about rejoining the abolitionist struggle in the United States. British abolitionists purchased his freedom in 1846, allowing Douglass to return to America without being reenslaved. Settling in Rochester, New York, a hotbed of reform, he began publishing *The North Star*.

Other black activists would stay overseas. Forming a black international, they kept constant pressure on American slaveholders. James Pennington escaped Maryland bondage and went to Britain, where he published *The Fugitive Blacksmith* in 1849. A celebrated lecturer, he spoke at antislavery rallies across Great Britain. William Craft and Ellen Craft fled their Georgia plantation after she disguised herself as a white master and he posed as a loyal slave. The ruse worked, and the Crafts made it to safe spaces in Pennsylvania and New England. They too settled in England, lectured on slavery's evil, and they later published a collective autobiography entitled "Running a Thousand Miles to Freedom." Whether at home or abroad, black abolitionists wanted the world to know that as long as slavery existed, America was a land of oppression.

Chapter 5

The abolitionist renaissance and the coming of the Civil War

Although abolitionists never enjoyed widespread popularity in the United States, they found that northerners were more interested in their critiques of slavery during the 1850s. The passage of a stronger fugitive slave law, which turned white citizens into would-be slave catchers, raised new questions about the slave power and allowed abolitionist arguments to resonate more deeply. The result was an abolitionist renaissance. From politics to pop culture, abolitionist ideas were diffused widely through American society. Even if most northerners did not join antislavery societies, the abolitionist struggle seemed ascendant in ways not seen since the late eighteenth century. And this had profound consequences for sectionalism, disunion, and civil war.

The Fugitive Slave Law and the abolitionist renaissance

The Fugitive Slave Law of 1850 inspired among many northerners a newfound sympathy for abolitionism. Part of a compromise that banned the slave trade in the District of Columbia and allowed California to enter the Union as a free state, the law mollified masters by cracking down on the perennial problem of runaways. It allowed federal commissioners to seize suspected fugitives and paid slave catchers a $10 bounty for every recovered runaway. It also empowered commissioners to deputize northerners as slave catchers, threatening fines and prison terms for those failing to comply. Though abolitionists condemned the law for its impact on blacks, whites understood that their liberties were threatened too.

Although masters used the law to recapture hundreds of runaways, many northern communities resisted it. After its passage in September, commissioners arrested James Hamlet in New York City and returned him to bondage in Maryland. Abolitionists raised funds for Hamlet's freedom, holding a big rally when he returned to New York. "Several thousand people, black and white, attended" the event, the *New York Tribune* reported, and there was a "strong spirit of resistance" to the "man stealing" law. According to longtime reformer Isaac Hopper, the Hamlet case "excited universal indignation at the vile law" and, for a change, made abolitionists heroes.

Several other cases proved the wisdom of Hopper's words. In Buffalo, abolitionists challenged officials who captured an alleged fugitive named Daniel in the summer of 1851. Arguing that he was a free man, a large group—led by blacks—gathered at the courthouse and tried to liberate Daniel. After abolitionists filed a writ of habeas corpus, Daniel was released and fled to Canada. In Syracuse, the so-called Jerry Rescue again found local citizens openly defying authorities. The case centered on William Henry, an escaped slave from Kentucky who lived under the alias "Jerry" before being seized by slave catchers in October 1851. Led by blacks, abolitionists stormed the prison and spirited Jerry away to Canada. For the next several years, local abolitionists celebrated Jerry's liberation day.

In 1860, still another high-profile case occurred in Troy, New York, where officials claimed Charles Nalle was a fugitive slave from Virginia. A throng of activists demanded Nalle's freedom, including Harriet Tubman, a former slave from Maryland who was already a noted figure on the Underground Railroad. On her way to an antislavery meeting in Boston, she heard about the

Nalle case and literally threw her body in the way of slave catchers twice to foil Nalle's return to bondage. The *New York Tribune* called it "The Slave Rescue at Troy."

So disruptive were black and white abolitionists along the Erie Canal corridor that Daniel Webster, the noted Massachusetts congressman, toured New York State with a special message: stop fugitive slave rescues or risk disunion. Even when Webster told a crowd in Syracuse that the city had become nothing but a "laboratory of abolitionism, libel and treason," local abolitionists refused to back down.

Every year, the Fugitive Slave Law faced major challenges somewhere in the North. In February 1851, Boston abolitionists stormed a prison holding Shadrach Minikins, a recaptured fugitive from Virginia, and sent him to freedom in Montreal. In the summer of 1853, slave catchers grabbed John Freeman in Indianapolis, Indiana, after a St. Louis master named Pleasant Ellington claimed that he was an escaped slave named "Sam." Remarkably, the federal commissioner allowed an investigation to ensue. While Freeman sat in jail, watched by an armed guard he had to pay for, his legal team produced witnesses showing that he was a free black man from Georgia and that Ellington had knowingly made a false claim. In fact, the real "Sam" had escaped to Canada, where he offered a deposition supporting Freeman's story.

In 1854, abolitionists liberated Joshua Glover from a Milwaukee jail and helped him escape to Canada. Glover had fled his St. Louis master and resettled in Milwaukee, where a small but active abolitionist community operated. After slave catchers found Glover, local citizens physically intervened on his behalf. Sherman Booth, a local politician and abolitionist, supported—but did not actually participate in—Glover's liberation, which led to his arrest for violating a federal law. The Wisconsin Supreme Court heard the case and released Booth after proclaiming that the Fugitive

Slave Law was unconstitutional—the only state court to do so. While he was retried and briefly spent time in jail, Booth eventually walked away.

Perhaps the most riveting rescue occurred in 1855, when abolitionists freed Jane Johnson and her two children on the Philadelphia waterfront. Johnson had been traveling with her master, North Carolina politician John Wheeler, who was on his way to a diplomatic post in Nicaragua. At a Philadelphia hotel, Johnson informed members of the black underground that she wished to be free. Abolitionists confronted Wheeler the next morning. As Quaker Passmore Williamson stood before Wheeler, black abolitionist William Still spirited Johnson's family away. Though Williamson spent several months in jail, he became a celebrity. Lucretia Mott, Frederick Douglass, and others visited him. Charges against Williamson were eventually dropped, and Still escaped punishment altogether. Rather stunningly, Johnson herself returned to testify in support of Williamson. She vanished again and was never caught.

Slave masters fumed again in 1858 when Ohio abolitionists foiled another attempted recovery. The Oberlin-Wellington Rescue began when slave-catchers tracked down an alleged Kentucky runaway named John Price in the college town well-known for its activism. Oberlin abolitionists pursued slave catchers to the nearby town of Wellington. Abolitionists eventually stormed the hotel where the slave catchers had barricaded themselves, liberating Price and sending him to Canada. Although federal charges were brought against thirty-seven people, Ohio authorities retaliated by arresting the slave catchers on a charge of kidnapping. After bargaining over their fate, most charges were dropped against Price's rescuers. Only two men did jail time: Charles Langston, a well-known black abolitionist and member of the Ohio Anti-Slavery Society, and white reformer Simeon Bushell. Langston became a hero, telling the court that the fugitive slave law "outrages every feeling of humanity." *The Cleveland Daily*

Herald agreed, writing that the "trial of these men for the crime of assisting a fellow man to escape life bondage...is a scene disgraceful to our country."

In each of these cases, fugitive slave rescues heightened debate over the willingness of northerners to support southern slavery. The most famous case of the decade—the return of Anthony Burns to Virginia bondage—showed that abolitionists gained public support for their antislavery work even when failing to free a fugitive. After he had been recaptured in Boston in May 1854, Burns was held in a local prison, where abolitionists staged a daring but unsuccessful raid to free him. Tragically, a white guard was killed in the melee—something that would normally have become the focus of public attention. But the opposite happened: As Burns was transferred to a ship bound for slave country, thousands of Bostonians lined the streets in protest. As businessman Amos Lawrence famously put it, "we went to bed one night old-fashioned, conservative, compromise Union [men]...and waked up stark mad abolitionists." Lawrence was not alone in questioning his previously moderate stand on slavery. Many abolitionists who saw themselves as peaceable citizens became militant opponents of the "man-stealing" law. No escaped slave was again recovered in Boston.

A literary renaissance

Fugitive slave conflicts revivified abolitionism. As concern over the law mounted in the North, abolitionists found themselves at the center of debates over civil liberties, the slave power, and the meaning of American democracy itself. For many people, abolitionists were truth-tellers, not rabble-rousers. More Americans than ever wanted to learn about the antislavery cause. Abolitionists met this demand with a flurry of new publications and artistic productions, making the movement relevant to American philosophy, literature, and even music. The Hutchinson Family Singers became one of the most popular vocal groups at midcentury for their heart-rending antislavery songs, including "The Fugitive's Song" (which was inspired by Douglass's autobiography).

Others meditated on slavery's negative environmental and economic consequences. Naturalist Henry David Thoreau became a more visible abolitionist commentator, offering a memorable condemnation of bondage in 1854 when he compared Massachusetts to a deadened landscape in the wake of the Anthony Burns affair. A member of the Concord Anti-Slavery Society, Thoreau linked abolitionism to his ecological views. Seeing all parts of American society as interconnected, he asserted that northerners were just as responsible for the ecology of bondage as southerners. Similarly, New York journalist Frederick Law Olmsted published *A Journey Through the Seaboard Slave States* (1856), which noted that both investors and immigrants refused to settle in the South because slavery discouraged free labor economics. Though he sometimes employed romantic racialism to make his case (arguing that enslaved people were virtual children who might require oversight in freedom), Olmsted inspired others to think more deeply about slavery's economic and environmental impacts.

John Trowbridge's novel *Neighbor Jackwood* (1856) used fiction to interrogate slavery's impact on the North. Trowbridge's tale focused on the plight of a runaway slave named Camille, who is protected by the Jackwood family after arriving in New England. As Trowbridge later explained, *Neighbor Jackwood* was based on the Anthony Burns imbroglio, which electrified everyone around him. The book went through several printings and was even made into a play.

Of course, no book was more impactful than Harriet Beecher Stowe's *Uncle Tom's Cabin*. Originally serialized in an abolitionist newspaper *The National Era*, the book sold well over one million copies after it was published in 1852. The novel spawned board games, trading cards, and plays, and Stowe went on an international speaking tour.

What made the book so popular and powerful? Stowe used collective biography to "enlist the sympathies" of the world in the antislavery cause, as she put it in a letter to Britain's Queen Victoria. The book's title character, a pious enslaved man named Tom, suffers at the hands of a heartless master—Simon Legree—who eventually kills him for the sin of believing that his Christian soul was equal to that of any white person. Even the prospect of death cannot vanquish Tom's spirit, which makes him the Christ-like sacrifice for the American sin of slaveholding—a Christian-centered theme well suited to nineteenth-century revivalists. Stowe made other characters pay for slavery's evil too, including Eva, an idealized child of a slaveholding family who buys Uncle Tom before having to sell him to pay debts. Eva, seemingly innocent of sin, is the only white character who seeks Tom's freedom. Stricken by disease, she passes away, leaving everyone devastated. Stowe's message: Slavery killed Eva just as it would destroy the American soul.

Despite its popularity, Stowe's novel did not appeal to everyone. No character in the book spoke for immediate abolition, frustrating some hard-core abolitionists. Moreover, the book used unflattering images of African American characters—including Uncle Tom, who always deferred to white power, and Topsy, an enslaved child whose wild behavior seemed inherent in her blackness. Stowe also flirted with colonization in yet-another storyline: the tale of George and Eliza Harris who escape slavery by fleeing to freedom in Canada. They then settle in the American Colonization Society's former colony of Liberia. Was this truly an abolitionist ending?

These concerns notwithstanding, Stowe's book remained a powerful indictment of slavery. As Stowe revealed in a follow-up book, *The Key to Uncle Tom's Cabin* ("facts for the people"), her novel was based on runaway slave ads, slave narratives, and stories of fugitive slave renditions. Having lived in the antislavery borderland of Cincinnati before settling in Boston, Stowe often heard about slave escapes. The daughter of a minister who married a preacher, she offered a literary sermon on bondage designed to shock, sadden, enrage, and ultimately galvanize Americans into becoming an antislavery congregation.

Though some ardent reformers believed she was not hard enough on slaveholders, the outcry from southern masters only deepened Stowe's abolitionist credentials. Slaveholder George Frederick Holmes offered a scathing review in *The Southern Literary Messenger*, blasting *Uncle Tom's Cabin* as "professedly a fiction." Stowe, he sneered, was a "politician in petticoats" whose novel lied about slavery and deserved nothing but derision. Holmes's review drew more attention to Stowe's book. As slaveholders now realized, they could not gag slavery debate in American culture.

Black abolitionist renaissance

Though abolitionists were gratified to see white northerners fight the slave power, the Fugitive Slave Law prompted the exodus of between ten and twenty thousand African Americans, mostly to British Canada. While they lived in vibrant "ex-pat" communities in Toronto, Hamilton, and other cities, blacks still found ways to attack American slavery. Mary Ann Shadd Cary, who hailed from a well-known black abolitionist family in Delaware, touted immigration to Canada as a boon to oppressed African Americans. As Cary put it in an 1852 pamphlet, "the inquisitorial inhumanity" of the Fugitive Slave Law proved that the United States was inhospitable to black freedom. In Canada, however, whites had an "innate hatred of American slavery" and free blacks had suffrage rights, access to public education facilities, and legal protections.

Cary joined forces with a talented editor who had once been enslaved in Maryland: Samuel Ringgold Ward. After living in New York, Ward moved north and joined the Canadian Antislavery Society. He and Cary published *The Provincial Freeman*, which reported on black abolitionist initiatives across the Atlantic world. When Ward traveled, Cary assumed the main editorial duties.

A superb writer and editor, she began printing letters from black abolitionist William Still, who became the leader of the Underground Railroad in Philadelphia. Still told readers that no law would stop fugitives from escaping American slavery and perhaps going to Canada. For that reason, Still reported, *The Provincial Freeman* "is read [in Philadelphia] with lively interest."

Both Cary and Still knew that Canadian exodus was part of a broader debate among black abolitionists at midcentury: was racial justice possible in slaveholding America? Martin Delany, a free black activist from western Virginia, scoffed at the notion. Espousing an early version of black nationalism, Delany convened the first black emigration convention in Cleveland in 1854 to encourage black exodus. As he observed in *The Political Destiny of the Colored People* (1852), throughout history oppressed communities achieved freedom and justice only by creating new settlements where they controlled economic, political, and social affairs. To achieve such results, blacks in America must build their own nation.

Despite Delany's forceful arguments, many African Americans rejected mass migration. Black abolitionists argued that they must remain allies to enslaved people struggling for freedom in the South and help overturn the broader system of racial oppression stifling northern society. Like revolutionary leader James Forten, they saw African Americans as a redeeming people who would transform the nation's moral fabric through waves of prophetic activism. Civil rights were American rights and African Americans had equal claims to them.

Frederick Douglass became the great exemplar of this civil rights position. He supported local struggles to integrate Rochester schools and used his various newspapers to battle the slave power. While he also supported workingmen's rights and women's equality (he attended the Seneca Falls convention in 1848), Douglass focused on a dual reconstruction of American society: slaying southern bondage and ending northern racism. He could do that only by remaining in the United States.

Douglass was not afraid to level harsh critiques of white abolitionists, from Garrison to Harriet Beecher Stowe. In his most famous speech, "What to the Slave Is the Fourth of July?" (1852), Douglass told a largely white crowd in Rochester that America had reached a crisis point. With both the Fugitive Slave Law and the domestic slave trade imperiling black lives, Douglass wondered why African Americans would ever celebrate July 4th. "Are the great principles of political freedom...extended to us?" he asked. The answer was clearly no. And so, he announced, "you may rejoice, I must mourn" on Independence Day. The speech condemned not only bondage but also white allies who did not match the activist convictions of the founders they celebrated. In an inspiring peroration, Douglass reminded abolitionists that the American Revolution was the result of action, not simply words.

In a less well-known but equally rousing speech a year later, Douglass returned to the Declaration of Independence as the touchstone of American equality. Reporting from a national convention of black activists in Rochester, Douglass told white Americans that we "address you as American citizens asserting their rights on their own native soil." "We are Americans," he concluded, and we demand nothing less than full civic equality. Until that time, he and black reformers vowed never to "repress the spirit of liberty within us, or...conceal...our sense of the justice and dignity of our cause."

Across the North, black abolitionists took up the civil rights standard by challenging school segregation, segregated accommodations, and racist thinking. In Philadelphia, African Americans began challenging segregated streetcars, while in

9. Like Douglass, Sojourner Truth saw photography as a truth-telling medium that would reveal the essential humanity of African Americans. In this Civil War image, Truth uses a piece of yarn to depict the United States on her lap. The implication is clear: black bodies will determine the fate of the nation. Truth herself filed for the copyright of this photograph.

Boston black activists sued to integrate city schools (in the case of *Roberts v. Boston*). In Ohio, John Mercer Langston became the first black lawyer to pass the state bar exam, joining his brother Charles in a variety of antiracist struggles. Again and again, black abolitionists reminded Americans that the struggle for racial justice was national in scope and one dedicated to the idea that the United States was, in essence, an abolitionist nation.

To make their case, black abolitionists embraced innovative visual technologies. For instance, both Douglass and Sojourner Truth utilized the new medium of photography to bolster black freedom claims. A photo did not lie, Douglass believed, and he linked the struggle for justice to what he called the "Age of Pictures." Little wonder that Douglass became one of the most photographed Americans of the nineteenth century: he wanted the objective lens of the camera to show the inescapable humanity of African Americans. Similarly, Sojourner Truth used photos to tell prophetic stories about herself and the nation. In one of her most famous photos, Truth sits in a chair with a piece of yarn draped over her lap in the form of the United States. While she poses as a respectable middle-class figure, the map implies that black bodies will not rest easily until slavery had been vanquished from the land. It was a stunning photograph, and it spoke volumes about the dynamic activism of black abolitionists before the Civil War.

Abolitionist politics and the abolitionist constitution

The rising visibility of black and white abolitionists made a mark on slaveholders. That became clear in November 1850, when a convention of southern leaders meeting in Nashville issued a series of resolutions warning northerners to control those "aggressive" abolitionists. Throughout the 1850s, "fire-eaters," a radical subset of proslavery politicians, threatened disunion as a way to push back.

Though their movement had grown, abolitionists remained on the periphery of political power. Just how would they destroy slavery? Like all movements for social change, they struggled to convert social discontent into coherent political action. One wing of the abolitionist movement still eschewed politics, touting disunion and radical individualism as a better way to overcome the slave power. John Jacobs, a fugitive slave and brother of slave narrator Harriet Jacobs, favored disunion because he thought it would force northerners to choose between slavery and freedom. Boston minister Theodore Parker supported ever-more-radical challenges to the Fugitive Slave Law. Parker told his congregation that he would "defend the fugitive with all my humble means and power," including physical force. Citing higher law principles—or the idea that there was a divine law above corrupt political authority—he asserted that a fugitive slave had "the same natural right to defend himself against the slave catcher" as anyone. "The man who attacks me to reduce me to slavery," he argued in the voice of the fugitive, "in that moment of attack alienates his right to life."

Unconvinced by such confrontational stands, Connecticut abolitionist Elihu Burritt proposed a new buyout plan of American bondage. Forming the National Compensation Emancipation Society (NCES) in 1857, he asked the federal government to pay slaveholders $250 for each liberated slave (with additional sums provided by the states) and $25 to each enslaved person (which they could use to settle domestically or migrate internationally). Though well under the going price for enslaved people, NCES advocates hoped that masters would see the "brotherly spirit" behind compensated emancipation and support the cause.

Building on earlier forays into politics, a succession of midcentury abolitionists also sought to deploy the U.S. Constitution against slavery. Inventor and lawyer Lysander Spooner argued that the federal government could not protect bondage because the Constitution did not use the term "slave" (the constitutional phraseology was "persons held to labor"). Spooner also believed that enslaved people could use writs of habeas corpus to challenge their detainment in bondage. Like Absalom Jones in 1799, Spooner believed that the Constitution supported black liberty over slaveholders.

By the 1850s many more reformers supported this position. William Goodell published a steady stream of books and pamphlets supporting an abolitionist Constitution. As he put it, "[i]f the Constitution requires us to support slavery, then the Constitution requires us to overthrow our own liberties, to declare war against universal humanity, to rebel against God, and incur his displeasure." But "if the Constitution be in favor of liberty and against slavery, then it is our duty and interest to wield it for the overthrow of slavery and the redemption of our country from the heel of the slave power." From his ministerial base outside Rochester, Goodell became an increasingly respected abolitionist theorist.

Indeed, Goodell's ideas pointed toward the "Freedom National" doctrine. Espoused by Massachusetts politician Charles Sumner, the doctrine viewed freedom as a national principle and slavery as a local one. As Sumner put it in his famous 1852 speech, "Freedom National, Slavery Sectional," "the Constitution was ordained, not to establish, secure, or sanction Slavery—not to promote the special interests of slaveholders—not to make Slavery national, in any way, form, or manner; but to 'establish justice,' 'promote the general welfare,' and 'secure the blessings of Liberty.' Here [in America] surely Liberty is national."

By interpreting the Constitution as a freedom document, Sumner, Goodell, and Spooner brought abolitionism into the American mainstream. Whereas for decades abolitionists had defined themselves as outsiders who challenged a corrupt political and constitutional order, midcentury reformers saw themselves as insiders who redeemed core American institutions. Hoping to correct "a popular belief" that slaveholders had eternal rights, Sumner excoriated anyone who argued that slavery was "a national institution." Wrong, he charged. Slavery was "a sectional institution...with which the nation has nothing to do." This policy of federal neglect would surely kill bondage.

Even Douglass repudiated his former Garrisonian beliefs and joined reformers who read the Constitution's preamble—"to establish justice" and "secure the blessing of liberty" for all Americans—as an abolitionist standard. Unsurprisingly, Douglass converted to political abolitionism too. Believing that abolitionists must use the political process to coerce slaveholders institutionally, he supported a range of third parties, including the Liberty Party. Douglass also helped launch the Radical Abolition Party (RAP), which called slavery unconstitutional, supported full citizenship for African Americans, and offered a stunning vision of interracial leadership by selecting black activist James McCune Smith as its inaugural convention chairman—something that would not happen again in party politics until the 20th century.

Though it gained little support, the Radical Abolition Party illuminated abolitionism's organizational dynamism. Far from a small band of New England radicals piously philosophizing about moral perfection, abolitionism was constantly experimenting with new political and social doctrines. As Goodell put it in *Slavery and Antislavery* (1852), there was "moral suasion" abolition, "political abolitionism," church-oriented abolition, and so on. And now that abolitionists were pushing into politics, slaveholders would find themselves pressed on more and more fronts.

The rise of the Republican Party

As abolitionists explored constitutional arguments against slavery and experimented with political parties, a new generation of antislavery statesmen entered the federal government: New

Hampshire's John P. Hale, Indiana's George Julian, Ohio's Benjamin Wade and Samuel Chase, and New York's William Seward. Bolstered by northern discontent with the Fugitive Slave Law, they supported restrictions on slavery in the West and opposed the slave power. Many of these statesmen also spoke of black freedom as a constituent part of America's past and future, making clear to slaveholders that they saw the union in ways that were fundamentally different from theirs.

Territorial debates over bondage pushed more northerners into the antislavery fold and emboldened antislavery statesmen. Though the issue had periodically roiled Congress, slavery's status in the West became a hot-button issue after the Mexican War ended in 1848. Abolitionists mobilized against the introduction of slaves in any conquered territory—a point politicians picked up. When Pennsylvania Democrat David Wilmot—no friend of abolitionists— proposed a law prohibiting slavery in new territories, slaveholders argued that bondage must be allowed to expand, or it would die. The Wilmot Proviso failed to pass but it put southern politicians on notice. After California entered the Union as a free state in 1850, Deep South politicians vowed not to lose another territorial battle.

Southern masters and their northern allies vindicated that vow with the Kansas-Nebraska Act. Introduced in 1854 by Illinois senator Stephen A. Douglas, a Democrat who courted southern support for a transcontinental railroad, the law repealed the Missouri Compromise and opened the Great Plains to slavery via the concept of popular sovereignty. No longer would slavery be prohibited above the 36°30' parallel; rather, a territory's population would decide slavery's fate. The act angered a broad swath of northerners. Stoked by abolitionists, northerners staged town hall meetings, lecture campaigns, fundraisers, and petition drives to oppose the Kansas-Nebraska Act. Abolitionists also sponsored free soil settlers who confronted slaveholders in territorial Kansas. The New England Emigrant Aid Society (NEEAS), a joint stock company dedicated to building a free

Kansas, helped populate abolitionist-friendly towns such as Lawrence.

Free soil settlers included Daniel and Merritt Anthony of Rochester. Brothers of Susan B. Anthony, who soon became a lecturer for the American Anti-Slavery Society, they had been abolitionists since the 1840s and counted Frederick Douglass as a friend. On their way to Kansas, Merritt recalled hearing one man threaten to tar and feather abolitionists. Undeterred, he and his brother settled in the embattled territory. Sending news of Kansas outrages back to the East, the Anthony brothers offered a vital connection to slavery debates out in the West.

The Anthony brothers were right to worry about their safety in Kansas. Abolitionists were not only verbally threatened but physically assaulted. In May 1856, the abolitionist stronghold of Lawrence was razed by a proslavery mob of roughly eight hundred people. In addition, "Border Ruffians" from Missouri consistently disrupted free state politics in Kansas. Abolitionist partisans in New York City sent "Beecher Bibles" to western emigrants: boxes of rifles named in honor of abolitionist minister Henry Ward Beecher. But that did little to quiet fears.

Kansas became a great recruiting tool for a new political party dedicated to fighting slavery's territorial expansion: the Republican Party. Formed in 1854, Republicans not only opposed slavery's westward expansion but also vowed to make American liberty the core of party identity—something that appealed to black as well as white reformers. The Republican Party platform of 1856 used the Declaration of Independence, with its guarantee of liberty as an American birthright, as the party standard. Moreover, Republicans promised to secure the liberty of conscience and press for embattled northerners—code words designed to appeal to potential abolitionist voters who felt that the Fugitive Slave Law had marginalized them. Republicans also supported free labor regimes, educational uplift, and the development of transportation infrastructure in the West.

The Republican Party replaced the Free Soil Party as the great hope of political abolitionists. Launched with great fanfare in 1848, the Free Soil Party focused on one major goal: restricting slavery's western growth. By stripping abolitionist planks from the old Liberty Party agenda, including emancipation in the District of Columbia, free soilers hoped to appeal to a much wider group of northerners. While it tallied 250,000 votes in the presidential election of 1848, the Free Soil Party created a rift among abolitionists. The party ran Martin Van Buren, slaveholder Andrew Jackson's confidant, as president. More broadly, many partisans of the Free Soil Party envisioned the West as a haven for white workers, not black settlers. When some settlers proposed a constitution prohibiting African Americans from living in the future state of Kansas, hard-core abolitionists registered alarm. Perhaps Garrison was right: popular politics and abolition did not mix.

Despite such concerns, perceptive reformers saw the Free Soil Party as a symbol of shifting allegiances in the North. Frederick Douglass, who attended the inaugural Free Soil convention in Buffalo, viewed it as a way station for voters frustrated by the slave power's influence on the two main political parties—Democrats and Whigs—yet still not ready to embrace emancipation. Douglass made an important point: members of the Free Soil Party were not monolithic. The party included politicians like Charles Sumner, who argued that limiting slavery's growth was a major step toward national freedom, and Samuel Chase, who defended fugitive slaves in Ohio.

Yet the Free Soil Party ultimately failed to keep pace with northern anger at the slave power. After a lackluster performance in the election of 1852, the party faded. Though it did not favor immediate emancipation in the South, the Republican Party was better able to capture northern frustration. While ardent abolitionists refused to support the Republican Party, moderates understood that northern opposition to the slave power was at an all-time high and they would be foolish to simply ignore Republican prospects. In 1854, anti-Kansas politicians captured dozens of seats in Congress. By tapping into northern resentment of the slave power, Republicans captured their first major political victory in 1856 when Massachusetts abolitionist Nathanial Banks was elected Speaker of the House. In the presidential election later that year, Republicans secured over more than one million votes (33 percent of ballots cast) and 114 electoral ballots. The party was a political juggernaut.

Though wary of Republicans, Frederick Douglass hoped for Republican "success." While dismayed that Republicans often rallied around the standard of "No more Slave States" rather "Death to Slavery," he knew that white northerners "will [still] not have [an abolitionist party]…and [so] we are compelled to work and wait for a brighter day, when the masses shall be educated up to a higher standard of human rights and political morality." The Republican Party was a step forward for the antislavery cause.

In fact, abolitionists found themselves on the same page as Republicans on several key occasions. In May 1856, Charles Sumner was viciously attacked in Congress after he gave a stunning speech accusing slaveholders of raping the "virgin" soil of Kansas. That prompted South Carolinian Preston Brooks to whip Sumner from behind with a cane. Trapped in his Senate desk and surrounded by southern politicians who would not let others intervene, Sumner was nearly beaten to death.

Brooks's attack on Sumner underscored a key abolitionist talking point: slaveholders acted as despots. Sumner was not simply an abolitionist martyr but a virtual white slave whose brutal whipping illustrated what bondsmen and women endured every day. Black abolitionists rushed to Sumner's defense. In Boston,

African Americans gathered at escaped slave Leonard Grimes's church to condemn slaveholders for their "brutal, cowardly and murderous assault…upon our distinguished Senator, Charles Sumner." The caning of Sumner raised the visibility and respectability of both abolitionists and the Republican Party.

The Supreme Court's *Dred Scott v. Sandford* decision in March 1857 created another bond between Republicans and abolitionists. In ruling against Dred Scott, an enslaved man who sued for his freedom after being taken into the Midwest, the Supreme Court hoped to quash slavery debate across the country and solidify slaveholders' rights nationally. Writing for the majority, Roger Taney (a Maryland slaveholder) dismissed Scott's freedom claim on two grounds: first, slaveholders' property rights were sacrosanct everywhere in American society, including free territories and states; and, second, African Americans were not U.S. citizens and, as he put it, had "no rights that a white man was bound to respect whatsoever."

Both abolitionists and Republicans responded vigorously to the *Dred Scott* decision, helping shape a sense of shared political destiny. Douglass railed against the opinion in speeches and editorials. "The testimony of the church, and the testimony of the founders of this Republic, from the Declaration downward, prove Judge Taney false," he told a New York City crowd in May. Though Garrison saw the decision as additional proof that American governance had been defiled by the slave power, he too was outraged by Taney's rhetoric.

Among Republicans, Abraham Lincoln took the lead in criticizing Taney's ruling. Like Douglass, he saw *Dred Scott* through the lens of history. "I had thought the Declaration contemplated the progressive improvement in the condition of all men everywhere," Lincoln commented, but the Taney decision reduced it to a mere political maneuver to support American independence. For Lincoln, as for Douglass, the Declaration remained the ultimate touchstone of American rights and values. The *Dred Scott* case violated that notion. Channeling Douglass, Lincoln even asked one audience about to celebrate the Fourth of July, "what for?" "But I suppose you will celebrate; and will even go so far as to read the Declaration," he continued. "Suppose after you read it once in the old fashioned way, [then] you read it once more with Judge Douglas' version," which focused on slaveholders' property rights and not human rights. How would it sound then? Clearly, Lincoln read Douglass's famous speech, agreeing that Taney's decision made July 4th a day to mourn and not celebrate.

When Lincoln asserted that "the negro is a man, that his bondage is cruelly wrong, and that the field of his oppression ought not to be enlarged," he won more friends among abolitionists. For Douglass, Garrison, and a range of others, the Republican Party seemed to be doing, at least in part, what they had done for decades: speaking truth to the slave power.

And that made the election of 1860 a truly historic event. It would be the first presidential election in which abolitionist values—if not policies—would become a key part of the nation's future.

Chapter 6
American emancipations: Abolitionism in the Civil War era

Even before the election of 1860, abolition made national headlines with John Brown's failed raid at Harpers Ferry. Though he hoped to foment a slave rebellion in western Virginia, Brown's raid ended with his capture and execution. While many Americans saw him as a fanatic, abolitionists viewed Brown as a flawed but conscience-driven man who rang an alarm bell about bondage. Like generations of slave rebels, Brown saw slavery as a perpetual war against enslaved people—a war that commanded rebels and their allies to fight back. Though still no fan of violence, Garrison told a Boston audience that "[w]e have been warmly sympathizing with John Brown all the way" to his death. He told abolitionists to use Brown's memory to do "the work of abolishing slavery."

Ironically, Brown's death put a spotlight on slaveholders too. While southern masters and their northern allies vilified abolitionists, some Republicans joined abolitionists in using Brown's memory to focus on slave power outrages. No one could have predicted that this tactic would lead to a civil war, or slavery's complete destruction, in the next few years. Then again, abolitionism had often taken unpredictable turns. The key point is that abolitionists were ready to exploit events to their advantage.

John Brown: abolitionist

Before he became a martyr, John Brown was an abolitionist Zelig: he was everywhere. Brown met with fugitive slaves in Canada, Free Soil settlers in Kansas, and abolitionist leaders in New York, New England, and Ohio. An old-style Puritan, Brown also believed in a modern brand of interracial equality. In May 1858, he and a large group of black expatriates gathered in Chatham, Ontario (British Canada), to draft a new government for a post-slavery America. This "Provisional Constitution" called U.S. bondage "a most barbarous, unprovoked, and unjustifiable war of one portion of its citizens upon another portion." The only remedy was immediate abolition and the creation of an interracial republic where blacks could be congressmen, presidents, and equal citizens. Brown carried the Provisional Constitution with him to Harper's Ferry.

Though he aided fugitive slaves in the Northeast, Brown's belief in physical confrontation with slaveholders took shape in the West. Settling in Kansas with his sons, Brown found free soilers outnumbered and outgunned. Chagrined at physical attacks on abolitionists dating back to Elijah Lovejoy, he vowed to fight back. In May 1856, after proslavery forces destroyed Lawrence, he led a group of vigilantes, who killed five men in retaliation. Known as the Pottawattamie Massacre, the event shocked the nation. But Brown was not publicly identified and headed back to the East.

By 1859, he saw slave rebellion as the only pathway to national emancipation. Brown informed a small circle of abolitionist leaders of his plan to attack a federal arsenal at Harpers Ferry, Virginia, and then head into the Appalachian Mountains, where his forces could make periodic attacks on southern plantations. After gathering an interracial group of twenty-one activists on a Maryland farm, Brown struck at Harpers Ferry on October 16. Though Brown's men briefly occupied the armory and took hostages from a nearby plantation, they soon retreated to a firehouse after being surrounded by local militia. Eventually, U.S. Army colonel Robert E. Lee captured Brown and several surviving raiders. On December 2, Brown faced the gallows.

While Lee and many slaveholders called him a "madman," many abolitionists hailed Brown as a prophet. "Who believes he is crazy now?" Henry David Thoreau asked in 1860, when slaveholders threatened to secede from the Union to protect slavery. The Philadelphia Female Anti-Slavery Society formally saluted Brown as a freedom fighter. In New York City, James McCune Smith hailed Brown as a hero.

Abolition, secession, and war

In the wake of Brown's raid, abolitionists found allies among Radical Republicans. Illinois Senator Lyman Trumbull subverted a Virginia congressman's investigation into Brown's raid by adding that a federal committee should also examine slaveholding outrages in Kansas. Ohio Republican Benjamin Wade agreed. While neither Wade nor Trumbull supported Brown's violent tactics, they depicted slaveholders (not abolitionists) as disturbers of the nation's peace. The abolitionist-Republican alliance, though tenuous, ensured that neither slavery nor slaveholders would escape scrutiny. This development worried southern masters.

Abraham Lincoln certainly believed that a lesson was to be learned in "old John Brown." Like other Republicans, he distanced himself from Brown's violent means while also sympathizing with his abolitionist ends. When Democrats blamed Brown's raid on the Republican Party, Lincoln countered that slave rebellions predated his party's formation. As he noted in his Cooper Union address, which launched Lincoln's presidential bid, the American founders wanted to put slavery on the path to elimination. He added that with no more slave states in the West, there could be no slave rebellions there.

Lincoln offered just enough antislavery substance to gain abolitionists' tentative support. "So far as the North is concerned," Garrison observed just before the 1860 presidential election, "a marvelous change for the better has taken place in public sentiment in relation to the anti-slavery movement," with most Americans acknowledging the essential "conflict between free institutions and slave institutions."

Lincoln's victory in November 1860 constituted a watershed in American politics. Securing a plurality of votes, he became the first presidential candidate to win on an avowedly antislavery platform. Though Republicans conceded bondage's legality in the South, they called expansion of slavery "political heresy," and they vowed to keep slavery out of new territories. In addition, the Republican Party platform conjured images of abolitionist founders: men who declared that "the normal condition of all the territory of the United States is freedom." Finally, highlighting antislavery readings of both the Declaration of Independence and the Constitution, the platform called egalitarianism the nation's enduring creed. Unsurprisingly, Lincoln was not allowed on the ballot in ten southern states.

Nevertheless, secession changed the political calculus for Lincoln, who pushed abolition aside to save the hallowed American union. By Lincoln's inauguration in March 1861, seven Deep South states had seceded and the allegiance of border states (which Lincoln needed) hung in the balance. Tellingly, every Deep South state defended secession by complaining about either fugitive slaves or abolitionist agitation—or both. Georgia secessionists noted that in "the last ten years we have had numerous and serious causes of complaint against our non-slave-holding confederate States with reference to the subject of African slavery." Mississippi proclaimed that "[o]ur position is thoroughly identified with the institution of slavery, the greatest material interest of the world" and one now threatened by abolitionist "hostility" in Washington. South Carolina chastised the North for its wanton disregard of the

Fugitive Slave Law. "For twenty-five years this [abolitionist] agitation has been steadily increasing," the state's secessionists declared, "until it has now secured to its aid the power of the ... [federal] Government." Only disunion would save slavery forever.

To avert disunion, Lincoln vowed to enforce the Fugitive Slave Law and sign a proposed Thirteenth Amendment protecting southern slavery in perpetuity. While Congress never passed the amendment, it illustrated the great odds abolitionists faced in 1861. Those odds grew greater after four more states—led by Virginia—joined the Confederacy in the wake of South Carolina's firing on Fort Sumter on April 12, 1861, and Lincoln's call for military mobilization.

The "secession winter" was one of the most dangerous times for abolitionists, who found angry northerners blaming them for disunion. Susan B. Anthony traveled across New York State vowing "No Union with Slaveholders" and "No Compromise" on slavery. She faced taunts and physical threats but she kept going. "Here we are ... alive after the Buffalo mob," she wrote after one close call. Despite opposition, "we must face it through" and fight for freedom.

The first emancipation: runaway slaves and black Republicans

Anthony's words served as a keynote to abolitionists' approach to the Civil War. From 1861 onward, they tried to turn sectional conflict into a grand emancipation struggle. Runaway slaves struck the first abolitionist blow by using secessionist chaos to flee to federal forts, where they could gain their freedom from "black Republicans." Since Kansas, proslavery politicians had derisively used that term to link Republicans to mass emancipation and interracial citizenship. With Lincoln's election, disunionists again stirred support for their cause by claiming that "black Republicans" would speedily liberate southern slaves. As Garrison noted, slaveholders "rave just as fiercely as though [Lincoln] were another John Brown, armed for Southern invasion and universal emancipation!"

Enslaved people took masters at their word and headed for "black Republicans." Even before military battles ensued, fugitive slaves fled to federal forts. In May, three enslaved people—Frank Baker, Shepard Mallory, and James Townsend—requested sanctuary at Fort Monroe, located outside Hampton, Virginia. The commander, General Benjamin Butler of Massachusetts, ingeniously declared them "contraband of war": illegal property used by slaveholders to fight the Union. Though a Democrat initially wary of emancipation, Butler's decree flowed from years of abolitionist legal maneuvering. When Colonel Mallory tried to reclaim the runaways, Butler held firm: runaway slaves would not be returned to the Confederacy. The Lincoln administration agreed. The first emancipation proclamation of the Civil War began with runaway slaves.

Abolitionists hailed Butler as a liberator. As the *Christian Recorder*, a leading African American journal that circulated through many black communities, explained, Butler was like Moses to enslaved people. While Butler's decree remained limited—enslaved people were in a liminal status between bondage and freedom—it made Union lines a new antislavery borderland. Just as Pennsylvania's gradual abolition act had unwittingly encouraged a wave of runaway activity on slavery's northern borderland, so too did Butler's contraband policy make Union installations a potential freedom line for enslaved people. By summer's end, nearly a thousand runaways resided at Fort Monroe. Fugitive slaves streamed to Union lines in New Orleans, Kentucky, South Carolina, and many other locales.

They inspired congressional passage of the First Confiscation Act in August 1861, which allowed military officials to seize contraband property employed against the Union. That law paved the way for a Second Confiscation Act in July 1862 authorizing federal officials to both seize Confederate property and liberate enslaved people in any disloyal area. Even before the Emancipation Proclamation, Confederates condemned these acts as attacks on slavery.

Lincoln worried that confiscation policies would undermine Union support in the loyal border states of Maryland, Kentucky, Missouri, and Delaware. Indeed, at the start of the war, Lincoln was anything but a great emancipator. In August 1861, he reversed General John C. Fremont's declaration that all slaves of rebel masters in Missouri were free. In the spring of 1862, he overturned Union general David Hunter's emancipation proclamation in the heart of the Confederacy, which would have liberated more than one million enslaved people in Florida, Georgia, and South Carolina. Abolitionists were infuriated by Lincoln's timidity.

These political setbacks notwithstanding, enslaved people kept arriving at Union lines. By the war's end, perhaps a half million enslaved people had fled southern plantations, creating a two-front war for southern masters: one against the Union, another against fugitive slaves.

The thrilling case of Robert Smalls symbolized enslaved people's ongoing efforts to have an impact on the war. In the spring of 1862, Smalls led his family out of bondage in Charleston Harbor by posing as a sea captain. He seized a Confederate ship, *The Planter*, and fooled the harbor patrol into letting him pass through. Narrowly escaping a barrage of shells, Smalls delivered the boat to stunned Union forces in the Atlantic. Coming at a challenging time for the Union army, Small's story recharged the northern war effort.

If the Civil War had somehow ended in 1862, its abolitionist heroes would have most certainly included Smalls and probably not Lincoln. Knowing that war did not automatically mean emancipation, abolitionists vowed to redouble their efforts.

The wartime abolitionist push

While enslaved people pushed from below, abolitionists used the press, pulpit, and lecture halls to call for emancipation in the public sphere. In May 1861, Frederick Douglass wrote that the simplest way to end the war "was to strike down slavery itself." If "freedom to the slave" was proclaimed "from the nation's capital," then the slaveholders' rebellion would die. Abolitionists heeded Douglass's call by meeting with Lincoln, petitioning Congress, and staging August 1st commemorations to remind Americans that Great Britain remained the world's most important abolitionist nation.

For much of the war, abolitionists posed as a loyal political opposition that supported the Union but agitated for slavery's destruction—including military emancipation. This represented a profound strategic shift in the movement and not all abolitionists supported it. Some radical reformers argued that emancipation must come through moral and not military means; others saw Lincoln as untrustworthy. But most abolitionists agreed that the movement must exploit this crucial moment in history: a civil war that might result in an emancipation peace.

To shape the Union effort, abolitionists became policy experts on the constitutional, legal, and international rationales for wartime emancipation. For instance, Boston abolitionist Mary Booth sought to influence Lincoln by translating Augustin Cochin's study of French emancipation into English. Booth believed that Cochin's text was timely, for the French abolitionist argued that Americans must abolish slavery for the good of Atlantic society.

Other abolitionists made intricate constitutional and political arguments for wartime emancipation. Moncur Conway's *The Golden Hour* detailed myriad routes to wartime abolition. Like others, Conway agreed with John Quincy Adams that the president, as "commander in chief" of the military during wartime, could abolish slavery to save the nation. In a remarkable passage, Conway asked readers to suppose that Lincoln had issued the following "proclamation" after the first "bomb…fell into Fort Sumter": "it is hereby declared that all the slaves in this country are free, and they are hereby justified in whatever measures they may find necessary to maintain their freedom." Failing presidential action, Conway noted, Congress had the power to "declare slavery abolished" through "the common defense and general welfare" clauses. Congress could even "impeach the president, if, to the detriment of the Republic, he should refuse" to abolish slavery under the War Powers clause. Moreover, military commanders could issue emancipation edicts to defeat the Confederacy. "In war, slavery is the strength of the South," Conway commented, and the federal government must attack it at every level.

In April 1862, Radical Republicans in Congress did just this by securing an emancipation law in the District of Columbia. One of abolitionists' long-standing policy goals, District emancipation earmarked $1 million in federal funds to liberate 3,150 enslaved people. District masters would be paid roughly $300 per emancipated slave while liberated blacks could get up to $100 if they departed the United States. Despite compensation, masters complained that District abolition was arbitrary because they did not get to vote on it.

Lincoln, emancipation, and abolitionism

Abolitionists rejoiced when Lincoln finally embraced emancipation. In July 1862, a desperate Lincoln told his cabinet, which included abolitionists Samuel Chase and William Seward, about plans to issue an emancipation edict as a wartime necessity. Importantly, no one tried to talk him out of it. After Union forces repelled General Robert Lee's forces at Antietam, Lincoln issued the Preliminary Emancipation Proclamation on September 22. It stated that if Confederate forces did not surrender by the end of

10. As this image shows, some people believed that Lincoln's Emancipation Proclamation liberated both enslaved people and white northerners from the tyranny of masters' rule.

the year, the Union would declare enslaved people in rebellious territories "forever free." When Confederates did not comply, the final Emancipation Proclamation took effect on January 1, 1863. Clearly, Lincoln acted for practical as well as moral reasons. As the

Union death toll rose, so too did complaints on the home front. In the midterm elections of 1862, anti-war Democrats would gain a significant number of seats in Congress. Lincoln knew he had to do something different.

While he came late to wartime abolitionism, Lincoln's Emancipation Proclamation illustrated his capacity to grow as a president—something abolitionists had hoped would occur. It also showed Lincoln's antislavery core: once he issued the Emancipation Proclamation, he did not rescind it. Henry Highland Garnet, who nearly gave up on the United States, hailed Lincoln's action as one of the greatest events in history. Even the radical abolitionist Parker Pillsbury, who constantly challenged Lincoln, supported the Emancipation Proclamation.

Lincoln's proclamation had major policy significance. It prevented foreign powers, namely Great Britain, France, and Russia, from recognizing the Confederacy, which was an avowed slaveholders' republic. At a practical level, the Emancipation Proclamation formalized Union protection of escaped slaves. Although rebellious slaveholders argued that Lincoln had no jurisdiction over them, they understood that his edict encouraged enslaved people to flee to Union lines. Masters took brutal steps to prevent this from happening. Jefferson Davis called the Emancipation Proclamation the "most execrable measure recorded in the history of guilty man."

In short, the Emancipation Proclamation was a bold move. It marked the first time any U.S. president supported southern emancipation, in war or otherwise. Lincoln's law was a form of creative destruction: the idea that moving forward required obliterating previous acts and beliefs. Prior to 1863, Lincoln favored gradual and compensated emancipation plans, including those linked to colonization. Faced with a devastating war, he blew past these gradualist limits. As one black correspondent put it,

Lincoln's Emancipation Proclamation proved that the world had changed.

Lincoln's edict would not have happened without abolitionist prodding and support. Throughout the war, local antislavery societies petitioned Congress to proclaim emancipation while the abolitionist press continually hammered Lincoln. A striking example comes from George Stephens, a free black correspondent for the *Weekly Anglo-African* newspaper who served as an aid to a Union officer. Stationed on the Virginia-Maryland border, Stephens watched runaway slaves stream into Union lines. Challenging Lincoln, he wrote that southern blacks were "a power that cannot be ignored."

On the international scene, abolitionists made the Confederacy a pariah. In Great Britain, a cadre of expatriate African Americans, including William Wells Brown, Sarah Parker Remond, and Ellen and William Craft, helped to convince Britons to stay out of the war. Working with British abolitionists, they focused on manufacturers and workers who grew worried that the lack of southern cotton would shutter English factories (the United States supplied more than 75 percent of England's raw cotton). Remond, a longtime member of the Salem Female Anti-Slavery Society and a traveling lecturer for the American Anti-Slavery Society, resettled in London and gave more than fifty speeches on the duty of the English people to oppose the Confederacy. As she put it in an 1862 speech, "[l]et no diplomacy of statesmen, no intimidation of slaveholders, no scarcity of cotton, no fear of slave insurrections, prevent the people of Great Britain from maintaining their position as the friend of the oppressed negro."

Black troops and abolitionism

With the Emancipation Proclamation in full force, many abolitionists supported the use of black troops. In late 1862,

Massachusetts abolitionist Thomas Wentworth Higginson led one of the inaugural regiments of former slaves: the First South Carolina Volunteers. Organized under the Militia Act of 1862, which allowed the use of black troops in special circumstances, the "First South" was comprised mostly of fugitive slaves. Under Higginson, who spent the previous decade helping the Boston Vigilance Committee protect fugitive slaves, the First South engaged in spying, raiding, and recruitment operations in South Carolina, Georgia, and Florida. In its first campaign, the regiment struck at rice plantations along the Georgia-Florida border, freeing more than 150 enslaved people, many of whom became Union soldiers.

The success of the First South, the First Kansas Colored Infantry, and other test regiments helped convince the Republican-dominated Congress to authorize black troops. In February 1863, Massachusetts organized the most famous black regiment: the 54th Massachusetts. With Frederick Douglass serving as a recruiter, it soon attracted more than one thousand enlistees, including many fugitive slaves. "Men of Color, To Arms!" Douglass urged in recruiting swings through New York, New England, and Pennsylvania. He was proud when two of his sons, Lewis and Charles, answered the call. In North Carolina, William Henry Singleton, an escaped slave who rushed to Union lines at New Bern, mobilized the First North Carolina Volunteers. It was commanded by a familiar name: James C. Beecher, the half-brother of Harriet Beecher Stowe.

Most black regiments were organized under the banner of the United States Colored Troops (USCT). Authorized in May 1863, the USCT comprised 175 regiments during the war. Nearly one hundred and eighty thousand African Americans fought in the Union army and twenty thousand in the Union navy. Perhaps three-quarters of these soldiers were former slaves. Black regiments fought in roughly four hundred battles; approximately forty thousand died, and a dozen black soldiers earned Purple Hearts for bravery. None of this would impress Confederate leaders, who passed a law treating captured black soldiers as slave rebels to be executed (similarly, white Union officers commanding black troops would be tried and executed). On the battlefield, Confederate soldiers often refused to treat blacks according to prevailing wartime conventions. At the Fort Pillow Massacre in Tennessee in April 1864, more than three hundred black troops were killed when Confederates—led by Nathan Bedford Forrest—refused to take African Americans as prisoners of war (surrendering whites were not attacked). Even in a brutal sectional war, such acts of ritual violence stood out.

Not all the action took place in the South. The largest training ground for black troops was Camp William Penn, located just outside Philadelphia. Set on land owned by longtime abolitionist Lucretia Mott, Camp William Penn opened in the summer of 1863. Roughly eleven thousand African American troops would pass through its gates. Black and white abolitionists were frequent visitors to Camp William Penn. On one occasion, Frederick Douglass told troops assembled there that they symbolized the highest aspirations of the new American Union.

Behind regimental lines, African American women played increasingly important roles in the war effort. At many U.S. forts and Union camps, self-emancipated women and children often outnumbered men. African American women worked as nurses, teachers, laundresses, cooks, and aides. Others taught in schools opening up in former slave country. Susie King Taylor, a young enslaved woman from Georgia who fled to Union lines in 1862, taught in a freedmen's school on St. Simons Island before serving as a nurse with the "First South." Taylor's indefatigable efforts won praise from Union officials.

Some black women became valued scouts and spies. Harriet Tubman, dubbed "General Tubman" by John Brown for her militant resolve, served with the Second South Carolina Volunteers, helping strategize an important attack on a

Confederate installation along the Combahee River in June 1863 that liberated hundreds of enslaved people. General David Hunter, who commanded the Southeast theatre for the Union Army, saluted Tubman's work.

Black troops created new optics for abolition. In the 1850s, African Americans were ridiculed in minstrel shows and unflattering songs. During the Civil War, they were increasingly celebrated as brave soldiers and patriotic Unionists. Thomas Nast's famous sketch, "A Negro Regiment in Action," symbolized the heroic character of black military service. Showing a charge by black troops that devolved into fierce hand-to-hand combat, the image was featured in *Harper's Weekly*, the most important magazine in the United States, in March 1863.

Harper's consistently covered the exploits of black troops, including the moving story of an enslaved man named Gordon who joined the Union army after running away. In the middle of 1863, the paper showed an image of Gordon's terribly scarred back to demonstrate "the degree of brutality which slavery has developed among the [southern] whites." Yet an accompanying image showed Gordon transformed by his military uniform. Gordon's tale offered a new storyline for the Union: just as he was liberated from bondage, so too would he help the Union liberate itself from the slave power. Even the headline was designed to transform white expectations about African Americans. Entitled "A Typical Negro," Gordon's story was that of a fighting black man who put his life on the line for the Union.

The iconography of black soldiers pressed up against the ongoing problem of racial inequality. In 1863, the 54th Massachusetts protested unequal wages in the Union army—a protest that lasted more than a year. Refusing lesser pay than whites ($10 per month versus $13), they argued that the federal government was duty bound to pay black soldiers equally. Not until June 1864 would the matter be rectified.

The pay dispute was just one area of concern for wartime abolitionists. On the northern home front, civic inequality remained the order of the day in many cities and towns. In Philadelphia, William Still protested rigid streetcar segregation that compelled even black soldiers to ride in separate areas. Despite organizing a petition campaign with more than 350 signatures (including white business, political, and cultural leaders), Still could not get private streetcar companies to change their policy. As Douglass put it, the seemingly "Christian city" of Philadelphia was anything but a model of brotherly love.

The worst example of northern prejudice came in the New York City draft riots of July 1863. As Union draft plans were put into place, working-class New Yorkers lashed out at African Americans and abolitionists. Over the course of several days, a largely Irish mob rampaged through the city, killing more than one hundred African Americans, including women and children. Only when the Army of the Potomac arrived from Gettysburg was the riot suppressed. This was no momentary issue. Bowing to white fears, New York did not raise its first black regiments until well after other states had, which black and white abolitionists attributed to powerful anti-abolitionist Democrats in state government. To deal with such wrongs, Peter Cooper—builder of Cooper Union, where Lincoln's presidential bid had taken shape—compelled members of New York City's elite to publicly support both emancipation and black troops. Cooper's activism notwithstanding, black and white abolitionists realized that they had to keeping fighting for freedom above the Mason-Dixon line.

Final abolition: The Thirteenth Amendment

The last major drive by abolitionists during the Civil War focused on securing a constitutional amendment to end slavery. By 1864, abolitionists, Radical Republicans, and Lincoln agreed that such an amendment was critical. Not only did the Emancipation Proclamation apply only to Confederate states, leaving roughly one million enslaved people and fugitive slaves in border states and Union camps, but the prospect of an alliance between conservative Unionists and repatriated masters might mean slavery's revival at some future date. Slavery needed to be eradicated constitutionally, not just militarily. With abolitionist support, Radical Republicans ensured that no emancipation backsliding would occur.

Ohio abolitionist James Ashley was the first politician to propose an antislavery amendment. The Republican congressman recalled debates over runaway slaves in the Ohio Valley of his youth. A friend and ally of Samuel Chase, he disliked compromise with slaveholders. In December 1863, he argued that an abolitionist amendment to the Constitution would seal slavery's fate.

Old debates about the ultimate ends of abolition complicated matters. While Ashley favored an amendment that banned bondage, Charles Sumner proposed one that linked black equality to constitutional abolition. A clever politician, Ashley knew that eradicating bondage would be tough enough, and he convinced others to support a stand-alone amendment on slavery. Lyman Trumbull refined the proposed amendment's language: "Neither slavery nor involuntary servitude, except as a punishment for a crime whereof the party shall have been duly convicted, shall exist within the United States, or any place subject to their jurisdiction." Like the Northwest Ordinance of 1787, upon which the amendment was based, Ashley and Trumbull made the amendment simple and direct.

Abolitionists backed the newly crafted Thirteenth Amendment with vigor. Using the publicity machine that they had perfected through decades of activism, they published editorials, held petition drives, and lectured far and wide on the amendment's vital nature. Anna Dickinson, a young Quaker abolitionist whose speaking career took off during the war, lectured Congress that slavery must be destroyed along with the Confederacy. The Women's Loyal National League, launched by Susan B. Anthony and Elizabeth Cady Stanton in 1863, gathered four hundred thousand signatures to pro-amendment congressional memorials. In churches and benevolent societies, African Americans supported the amendment too.

Abolitionist backing was critical, for the election of 1864 proved that emancipation remained embattled in national politics. Former Union general George B. McClellan ran against Lincoln as a peace Democrat who vowed to return the nation to its pre-1860 social and political order. No fan of emancipation, McClellan had a special animus against Lincoln, who had removed him from high command. Though McClellan appeared to have a real shot at winning, Sherman's conquest of Atlanta settled matters and secured the election for Lincoln.

The election showed that abolitionism, military success, and Republican politicking were tightly linked. Discussion of the proposed Thirteenth Amendment stopped at key moments in 1864. While Ashley and his Republican colleagues pushed the amendment through the Senate in April, the House refused to follow suit in June. Clearly Union Democrats (and even some conservative Republicans) were waiting to see what happened on the battlefield before moving forward.

After Lincoln's victory in November, Ashley and his allies resumed the amendment push. With some ingenious parliamentary maneuvering, Ashley and his Republican colleagues targeted January 31, 1865, as the day to finalize support for the amendment in the House of Representatives (it had previously passed in the Senate). Getting just enough Democrats on their side for a super majority, which passage of amendments required, Republicans prevailed: 119 in favor, 59 opposed. As a poem in *Harper's* soon put it, America was now "free."

Abolitionists rejoiced. For the first time in their lives, slavery would be illegal. Countless abolitionists and freedom fighters never lived to see national emancipation: Denmark Vesey, Richard Allen, David Walker, Henry David Thoreau, Theodore Parker, Anthony Burns, and thousands upon thousands of enslaved people. Even Lincoln, who never joined an abolition society but became perhaps the greatest abolitionist statesman of the age, died before the Thirteenth Amendment was ratified by the states in December (when Georgia approved it). His assassin, John Wilkes Booth, fired one last shot at Lincoln's emancipation war. Booth recoiled at the prospect not only of Confederate defeat but also of an abolitionist victory.

By the time Booth struck down Lincoln, black troops had helped end the Civil War in Virginia. In April 1865, roughly two thousand African Americans fought at Appomattox, ensuring that Robert E. Lee would not slip away. The irony was powerful: only a few years before, John Brown and his interracial band sought to foment a slave uprising in western Virginia. They were captured by Lee and the U.S. Army. Now that same army included tens of thousands of runaway slaves, some of whom forced Lee's rebels to surrender in western Virginia.

In Charleston, black and white abolitionists took particular delight in slavery's demise. Black troops marched into secession's longtime capital singing "John Brown's Body"—a Union anthem based on an old slave spiritual. Greeted by a throng of enslaved people in February 1865, they took the city in the name of the new Union. "Marching On!" *Harper's Weekly* declared. In March, Charleston's black community buried a coffin marked "slavery." South Carolina had landed more slave-trading vessels than any other American colony or state; now the state witnessed slavery's last rites.

In April, longtime abolitionists William Lloyd Garrison and Henry Ward Beecher raised the U.S. flag at Fort Sumter. When the Civil War started four years earlier, that flag represented a republic still very much dedicated to slavery. Now it symbolized the new birth of freedom that promised equality and justice for all Americans. For the first time in his life, Garrison recalled, he felt proud to be an American.

In Texas, news of slavery's demise would not reach enslaved people for two more months. On June 19, 1865, Union general Gordon Granger arrived in Galveston with General Orders Number 3, which declared that, in accord with Lincoln's Emancipation Proclamation, "all slaves are free." While black people celebrated, the first "Juneteenth" Proclamation was also accompanied by fear. Until ratification of the Thirteenth Amendment by the states was complete, African Americans worried that slaveholders would retaliate against liberated slaves. If it had taken years to hear about the Emancipation Proclamation in Texas, where Deep South masters had gathered as a last redoubt of bondage, perhaps black freedom would always be a precarious proposition. Even today, Juneteenth celebrations serve as a potent reminder that we can never take freedom for granted.

Epilogue: Abolitionist endings in the Atlantic world ... and new beginnings

In the final decades of the nineteenth century, American abolitionists began writing memoirs, histories, and reminiscences of the grand struggle for freedom. Part of a battle over Civil War memory, they sought not only to claim a piece of history but also to combat Lost Cause narratives that already denigrated emancipation. Even though American slavery was history, abolitionist battles continued.

Across the Atlantic world abolitionists realized that their struggle was not over. British abolitionists focused on the perils of illegal slave trading, while Iberian and Latin American abolitionists renewed their struggle against bondage itself. In the U.S. South, abolitionists fought against new forms of discrimination that approximated slavery. Like a century before, abolitionists found themselves on the front lines of battle.

Unfinished business: American abolition after the Civil War

The end of the Civil War prompted fierce debate among abolitionists about the future of their movement. Did slavery's demise end their struggle? While members of the Pennsylvania Anti-Slavery Society and the American Anti-Slavery Society vowed to remain active until black voting rights had been achieved, no less a figure than Garrison saw slavery's destruction as a reason to stop *The Liberator*. Though he would fight for black equality, Garrison issued his last paper on December 31, 1865.

While jubilant at slavery's demise, black leaders worried that Confederate amnesty and northern apathy after the war would allow new forms of white supremacy—peonage, sharecropping, prison labor—to prosper. Already by 1866, southern black codes restricted African American movement and tied blacks to onerous labor contracts with former masters. "The Negroes are free as to their chains," John Sella Martin, who had escaped Georgia bondage and worked in black abolitionist circles from Buffalo to Chicago before becoming a missionary, said, "but everywhere their prospects are darkened by prejudice and proscription." In the North, segregation survived the war, challenging Lincoln's promise of a "New Birth of Freedom."

Even before the Civil War ended, black abolitionists mobilized against racial retrenchment. In 1864, they formed the National Equal Rights League (NERL) in Syracuse, New York. The NERL supported full citizenship, voting rights, and equal educational opportunity. "We are here to promote the freedom, progress, elevation and perfect enfranchisement of the entire colored people of the United States," Douglass observed. During Reconstruction, NERL branches appeared from New England to North Carolina. With a new generation of black leaders emerging—George Ruffin of Massachusetts, Octavius Catto of Pennsylvania, Blanche K. Bruce of Mississippi—the activist ranks seemed rejuvenated. Black abolitionist Philip Bell took the struggle to California, where he published *The Elevator* in the late 1860s. Based in San Francisco, the paper's rallying cry was "Equality Before the Law." That standard shaped black abolitionist struggles from the Atlantic to the Pacific.

No issue became more important than voting rights. "Give us suffrage and you may rely upon us to secure justice for ourselves," African Americans in Norfolk, Virginia, declared in June 1865.

Noting that voting was an emblem of "full citizenship," as well as a pathway to economic and political uplift, they demanded "equal suffrage in particular." In 1867, Radical Republicans responded by passing two important laws: the first granted black male suffrage in Washington, DC, and the second required former Confederate states to let black men vote. Congressional passage of the Fourteenth Amendment, which provided due process and "equal protection of the laws" to all citizens, further enhanced black claims to full citizenship. But the Fifteenth Amendment, passed in 1870, secured voting rights for black men across the land. Even northern states like Pennsylvania that had disfranchised blacks before the Civil War allowed African American men to vote.

With hundreds of thousands of African Americans on the voting rolls, black officials entered politics at the local, state, and national levels. Nearly two thousand African Americans held office during Reconstruction, including congressmen, governors, and state legislators. Convinced that another essential plank of the abolitionist cause had been attained, the American Anti-Slavery Society closed in 1870.

Upset that suffrage had not been universal, some female abolitionists bitterly opposed the Fifteenth Amendment. Both Susan B. Anthony and Elizabeth Cady Stanton broke ranks from Douglass and other African American reformers. This division was nastier than in the 1840s and took many years to heal, though Douglass and Anthony did eventually mend fences. Indeed, Douglass and other black abolitionists still pushed for women's suffrage too. Yet the 1870 split served as a potent reminder that abolitionism remained a crucible of democratic debate.

By that time, American abolitionists were already branching out into other reform causes. Just as Susan B. Anthony fought for women's suffrage, so too did Henry Ingersoll Bowditch, who spent decades in the Boston antislavery movement, embrace public health reform, tenement house reform, and immigrants' rights struggles. Lyman

Trumbull, the Illinois congressman who co-authored the Thirteenth Amendment, supported environmentalism (he fought for the Yellowstone National Park Law in 1872) and labor rights (he defended socialist organizer Eugene Debs in the wake of the Chicago Pullman Strike in 1894). Michigan abolitionist Laura Haviland, who once helped runaway slaves in Detroit, launched freedom schools for African Americans in Kansas City.

Each of these abolitionists believed deeply in social justice and saw the antislavery movement as a laboratory of reform. The toolbox of activist methods they learned in the abolitionist movement proved efficacious elsewhere. Indeed, abolitionist protest influenced generations of reformers. Upton Sinclair's *The Jungle*, a riveting exposé of Chicago industrial life, was modeled on *Uncle Tom's Cabin*. while modern civil rights activists referred to themselves as "neo-abolitionists." Even civil disobedience tactics, which influenced both Gandhi and Martin Luther King Jr., had abolitionist antecedents in both David Ruggles and Henry David Thoreau.

Completing Atlantic abolition

Abolitionists continued to push for emancipation across the Atlantic world. A global meeting of abolitionists in France in 1867 noted that, while the American Civil War had defeated the world's largest slave regime, bondage thrived in the Spanish Caribbean and Brazil. In both locales, a new generation of abolitionists challenged bondage. Less attuned to evangelical and crusading sentiments than their Anglo-American counterparts, Iberian and Latin American abolitionists nevertheless saw emancipation as an essential part of both modernization and Atlantic liberalism.

When reformers launched the Spanish Abolition Society (SAS) in Madrid in 1865, roughly half a million enslaved people could be found in Cuba and several hundred thousand in Puerto Rico. (Spain had abolished bondage within its borders in 1837.)

Comprised of intellectuals, politicians, and writers on both sides of the Atlantic, the SAS believed that colonial abolition would facilitate economic and political modernization in the Spanish Empire.

International pressures influenced Spanish and Cuban abolition struggles too. British efforts to end the slave trade in the Spanish Caribbean (part of diplomatic agreements between the two nations in 1835 and 1845) spawned a renewed focus on slavery. *Uncle Tom's Cabin* was republished in several Spanish editions and turned into a popular play after midcentury. In 1868, rebels launched an independence struggle in eastern Cuba that compelled both colonial and metropolitan officials to seek the allegiance of enslaved people. Known as the Ten Years' War, it drove a wedge into proslavery defenses. Rebel leaders (including planters) outlawed bondage to gain enslaved peoples' support, while Iberian abolitionists argued that emancipation would convince slaves to back Imperial Spain.

In this chaotic environment, Spanish officials enacted the Moret Law of 1870. Named for politician Segismundo Moret, it freed enslaved people born after 1868 but bound them to their owners until age twenty-one. The law also liberated enslaved people over sixty and those owned by the Spanish government. Its most ringing clause proclaimed that "all slaves who have served under the Spanish flag, or in any way have aided the troops during the current insurrection in Cuba, are declared free."

The Moret Law proved to be the first shot in an ongoing battle for universal emancipation in colonial Spain. In Puerto Rico, several key abolitionists pushed for a speedier emancipation process, including Ramón Emeterio Betances, who was previously exiled for supporting black freedom; Julio L. de Vizcarrondo, a former slaveholder who embraced abolition; and José Julián Acosta, an educator, intellectual, and newspaper publisher who was imprisoned for allegedly supporting independence struggles.

Each of these men traveled internationally, read antislavery literature from across the Atlantic world, and/or interacted with global reformers. They also heeded emancipation calls from enslaved people. In 1873, this alliance helped convince the Spanish government to end slavery in Puerto Rico. It took longer but a similar push ended Cuban slavery in 1886.

In Brazil, an abolitionist renaissance chipped away at slavery. After a British crackdown, Brazil banned the slave trade in 1850. To keep pace with labor needs, Brazilians turned to immigration, which reduced but did not eliminate slavery's power. Emboldened, abolitionists convinced Brazil to pass the Rio Branco Law, which promised freedom to enslaved people born after 1871 (though again former slaves were tied to their masters until early adulthood). Like Spanish abolition, the Brazilian movement was diverse, including such notable figures as Joaquim Nabuco, who hailed from an elite family but long favored emancipation, as well as mixed-race activists like Francisco José do Nascimento and José do Patrocínio, both of whom rallied against the iniquities of slavery in a modernizing age. Nabuco's 1883 book, *O Abolicionismo* (Abolitionism), decried slavery's corrosive power and argued that Brazilians must embrace full freedom for enslaved people. After several states passed final emancipation decrees, Brazil adopted the so-called Golden Law in 1888 banning bondage forever. As a Portuguese colony and then independent nation, Brazil had imported more slaves than any other Atlantic polity. Now black freedom reigned across the Atlantic world.

The long civil rights movement or the eternal emancipation struggle?

In reality, as W. E. B. DuBois would soon note in *The Souls of Black Folk* (1903), abolition merely positioned reformers for broader battles over race prejudice in the twentieth century. Born in 1868 in Massachusetts, DuBois grew up hearing tales about southern Reconstruction's grand hopes and epic failures. One of the worst reminders that racism had not died in the United States came when DuBois was a young boy: The Colfax massacre of April 1873. After a disputed election for governor in this small Louisiana town, Democrats attacked African Americans guarding the Colfax courthouse. Several dozen blacks were killed. Like anti-abolitionist violence of the 1830s, rioters targeted not just people but a cause: black voting rights. A few years earlier, black educator and activist Octavius Catto lost his life under similar circumstances. In October 1871, he was gunned down in Philadelphia after voting in a local election.

In response to such incidents, black abolitionists staged nearly thirty conventions in the 1870s. In 1879, a national convention of African American leaders gathering in Nashville, Tennessee, noted that unfair labor and educational conditions still prevailed across the South (and even in the North), limiting black citizenship and equality. "Obstacles have been constantly thrown in our way to obstruct and retard our progress," they asserted. And the formal end of Reconstruction in 1877—which saw the removal of federal troops from the South—allowed a thoroughly "intolerant spirit" to take root among political leaders in most southern states.

As a new century loomed, Frederick Douglass worried that abolitionism had been betrayed. As he put it in his last major speech, "The Lessons of the Hour" (1894), a bravura performance at Metropolitan AME Church in Washington, DC, a terrible rise in "race prejudice"—from legal segregation to lynch law—only proved that black freedom remained a precarious proposition.

As always, Douglass's spirit was buoyed by activism, in this case the work of Ida B. Wells. The daughter of slaves, Wells was a crusading journalist whose anti-lynching campaign revivified the struggle for racial justice in the 1890s. Douglass was proud to work with her. "Power concedes nothing without demand," Douglass once observed. "It never has and it never will." In Ida B. Wells, he saw that old abolitionist spirit of agitation gloriously renewed.

References

Introduction

Baptist, Edward. *The Half Has Never Been Told: Slavery and the Making of American Capitalism*. New York: Basic Books, 2014.

Bender, Thomas, ed. *The Antislavery Debate*. Berkeley: University of California Press, 1992.

Blackburn, Robin. *American Crucible: Slavery, Emancipation and Human Rights*. London: Verso, 2011.

Delbanco, Andrew. *The Abolitionist Imagination*. Cambridge, MA: Harvard University Press, 2012.

Douglass, Frederick. *Life and Times of Frederick Douglass*. Minneapolis: Zenith Books, 2015.

Drescher, Seymour. *Abolition: A History of Slavery and Antislavery*. New York: Cambridge University Press, 2010.

Hahn, Steven. *The Political Worlds of Slavery and Freedom*. Cambridge, MA: Harvard University Press, 2009.

Jeffrey, Julie Roy. *The Great Silent Army of Abolitionism: Ordinary Women in the Antislavery Movement*. Chapel Hill: University of North Carolina Press, 1998.

Kendi, Ibram X. *Stamped from the Beginning: The Definitive History of Racist Ideas*. New York: Nation Books, 2017.

Oakes, James. "The Real Problem with White Abolitionists," *Jacobin*, August 5, 2014. www.jacobinmag.com.

Quarles, Benjamin. *Black Abolitionists*. New York: Da Capo, 1991.

Sinha, Manisha. *The Slave's Cause: A History of Abolition*. New Haven, CT: Yale University Press, 2016.

Sweet, James H. *Domingos Alvares, African Healing, and the Intellectual History of the Atlantic World*. Chapel Hill: University of North Carolina Press, 2013.

"The Rev. [John] Sella Martin," British and Foreign Anti-Slavery Society. "Special Report of the Anti-Slavery Conference held in Paris...in August 1867." London: W. M. Watts, 1867.

Chapter 1

Brown, Vincent, et al. *Slave Revolt in Jamaica, 1760–61*. http://revolt.axismaps.com/.

Davis, David Brion. *The Problem of Slavery in the Age of Revolution, 1770–1823*. New York: Oxford University Press, 1999.

Eltis, David, et al. Voyages: The Trans-Atlantic Slave Trade Data Base. http://www.slavevoyages.org/.

Finkelman, Paul. "Three-Fifths Clause: Why Its Taint Persists." *The Root*, February 26, 2013. https://www.theroot.com/three-fifths-clause-why-its-taint-persists-1790895387.

Jackson, Maurice. *Let This Voice Be Heard: Anthony Benezet, the Father of Atlantic Abolitionism*. Philadelphia: University of Pennsylvania Press, 2010.

Nash, Gary B. *Race and Revolution*. Lanham, MD: Rowman and Littlefield, 1990.

Newman, Richard S. *The Transformation of American Abolitionism: Fighting Slavery in the Early Republic*. Chapel Hill: University of North Carolina Press, 2002.

Rediker, Marcus. *The Fearless Benjamin Lay*. Boston: Beacon Press, 2017.

Resendez, Andrés. *The Other Slavery: The Uncovered Story of Indian Enslavement in America*. New York: Mariner Books, 2017.

Soderlund, Jean R. *Quakers and Slavery: A Divided Spirit*. Princeton, NJ: Princeton University Press, 2014.

Wise, Steven M. *Though the Heavens May Fall: The Landmark Trial That Led to the End of Human Slavery*. New York: Da Capo, 2006.

Wolf, Eva Sheppard. *Race and Liberty in the New Nation: Emancipation in Virginia from the Revolution to Nat Turner's Rebellion*. Baton Rouge: Louisiana State University Press, 2006.

Chapter 2

Bernier, Celeste-Marie. *Characters of Blood: Black Heroism in the Transatlantic Imagination*. Charlottesville: University of Virginia Press, 2012.

Dubois, Laurent. *Avengers of the New World: The Story of the Haitian Revolution*. Cambridge, MA: Harvard University Press, 2005.

Egerton, Douglas. *Gabriel's Rebellion*. Chapel Hill: University of North Carolina Press, 1993.

Forbes, Robert. *The Missouri Crisis and Its Aftermath*. Chapel Hill: University of North Carolina Press, 2007.

Hinks, Peter. *To Awaken My Afflicted Brethren: David Walker and the Problem of Antebellum Slave Resistance*. University Park: Pennsylvania State University Press, 1996.

Johnson, Walter. *River of Dark Dreams: Slavery and Empire in the Cotton Kingdom*. Cambridge, MA: Harvard University Press, 2013.

National Archives. *The Meaning and Making of Emancipation*. (An ebook featuring Absalom Jones's 1799 antislavery petition). https://prologue.blogs.archives.gov/2012/12/04/emancipation-proclamation-petitioning-for-freedom/.

Newman, Richard S. *Freedom's Prophet: Bishop Richard Allen, the AME Church, and the Black Founders*. New York: New York University Press, 2009.

Newman, Richard, and Roy Finkenbine, eds. "Black Founders: A Roundtable." *The William and Mary Quarterly* 64.1 (January 2007); and web supplement: http://oieahc.wm.edu/wmq/Jan07/supplement.html.

Schmidt-Nowara, Christopher. *Slavery, Freedom and Abolition in Latin America and the Atlantic World*. Albuquerque: University of New Mexico Press, 2011.

Chapter 3

Abzug, Robert. *Theodore Dwight Weld and the Dilemma of Reform*. New York: Oxford University Press, 1982.

Breen, Patrick H. *The Land Shall Be Deluged in Blood: A New History of the Nat Turner Revolt*. New York: Oxford University Press, 2016.

Drescher, Seymour. *The Mighty Experiment: Free Labor vs. Slavery in British Emancipation*. New York: Oxford University Press, 2004.

Egerton, Douglas, and Robert Pacquette. *The Denmark Vesey Affair: A Documentary History*. Gainesville: University Press of Florida, 2017.

Heyrick, Elizabeth. "Immediate, Not Gradual, Abolition." Internet Archive: https://archive.org/details/oates71082024.

Hodges, Graham. *David Ruggles: A Radical Black Abolitionist and the Underground Railroad in New York City*. Chapel Hill: University of North Carolina Press, 2010.

Kraditor, Aileen S. *Means and Ends in American Abolitionism: Garrison and His Critics on Strategy and Tactics, 1834–1850*. Chicago: Ivan R. Dee, 1989.

Lerner, Gerda. *The Grimké Sisters from South Carolina*. Reprint, New York: Oxford University Press, 1998.

Meyer, Henry. *All on Fire: William Lloyd Garrison and the Abolition of Slavery*. New York: W. W. Norton, 2008.

Robertson, Stacey. *Hearts Beating for Liberty: Women Abolitionists in the Old Northwest*. Chapel Hill: University of North Carolina Press, 2010.

Stewart, James Brewer. *Holy Warriors: The Abolitionists and American Slavery*. Reprint, New York: Hill and Wang, 1997.

Tomek, Beverly. *Pennsylvania Hall: A Legal Lynching in the Shadow of the Liberty Bell*. New York: Oxford University Press, 2013.

Weld, Theodore Dwight. *American Slavery As It Is*. Internet Archive: https://archive.org/details/americanslavery1839weld2.

Chapter 4

Andrews, William, and Henry Louis Gates Jr., eds. *Slave Narratives*. New York: Library of America, 2000.

Brooks, Corey. *Liberty Power: Antislavery Third Parties and the Transformation of American Politics*. Chicago: University of Chicago Press, 2016.

Davis, Charles T., and Henry Louis Gates Jr., eds. *The Slave's Narrative*. New York: Oxford University Press, 1991.

Dubois, Laurent. *Haiti: The Aftershocks of History*. New York: Picador, 2013.

Finkelman, Paul, ed. *Defending Slavery: Proslavery Thought in the Old South; A Brief History with Documents*. New York: Bedford/St. Martin's, 2003.

Jones, Howard. *Mutiny on the Amistad*. New York: Oxford University Press, 1997.

"Lectures of George Thompson" (Boston, 1836). Internet Archive: https://archive.org/details/lecturesgeorge00thomrich.

McKivigan, John R. *The War against Proslavery Religion: Abolitionism and the Northern Churches*. Ithaca, NY: Cornell University Press, 2009.

Rael, Patrick. *Black Identity and Black Protest in the Antebellum North*. Chapel Hill: University of North Carolina Press, 2002.

Salerno, Beth. *Sister Societies: Women's Antislavery Organizations in Antebellum America*. DeKalb: Northern Illinois University Press, 2005.

Stauffer, John. *Giants*. New York: Twelve Publishers, 2008.

Sterling, Dorothy. *Ahead of Her Time: Abby Kelley and the Politics of Antislavery*. New York: W. W. Norton, 1991.

Wyatt-Brown, Bertram. *Lewis Tappan and the Evangelical War against Slavery*. Reprint, Baton Rouge: Louisiana State University Press, 1997.

Chapter 5

Campbell, Stanley. *Slave Catchers: Enforcement of the Fugitive Slave Law, 1850–1860*. New York: W. W. Norton, 1972.

Freehling, William W. *The Road to Disunion*. Vol. 1, *Secessionists at Bay*. New York: Oxford University Press, 1990.

Gac, Scot. *Singing for Freedom: The Hutchinson Family Singers and the 19th-Century Culture of Reform*. New Haven, CT: Yale University Press, 2007.

Oakes, James. *Freedom National: The Destruction of Slavery in the United States*. New York: W. W. Norton, 2014.

Reynolds, David S. *Mightier Than the Sword: Uncle Tom's Cabin and the Battle for America*. New York: W. W. Norton, 2011.

Rhodes, Jane. *Mary Ann Shadd Cary: The Black Press and Protest in the Nineteenth Century*. Bloomington: Indiana University Press, 2011.

Stauffer, John, Zoe Trodd, and Celeste-Marie Bernier, eds. *Picturing Frederick Douglass*. New York: Liveright, 2015.

Still, William. *The Underground Railroad*. Philadelphia, 1872.

Washington, Margaret. *Sojourner Truth's America*. Urbana: University of Illinois Press, 2011.

Yellin, Jean Fagin. *Harriet Jacobs: A Life*. New York: Civitas Books, 2003.

Chapter 6

Berlin, Ira. *The Long Emancipation: The Demise of Slavery in the United States*. Cambridge, MA: Harvard University Press, 2015.

Blackett, Richard. *Divided Hearts: Britain and the American Civil War*. Baton Rouge: Louisiana State University Press, 2000.

Cooper, William J., Jr. *Jefferson Davis, American*. New York: Vintage, 2001.

Egerton, Douglas. *Thunder at the Gates: The Black Civil War Regiments That Redeemed America*. New York: Basic Books, 2016.

Guelzo, Allen. *Lincoln's Emancipation Proclamation*. New York: Simon and Schuster, 2006.

Harper's Weekly online archives.

Kachun, Mitch. *Festivals of Freedom*. Amherst: University of Massachusetts Press, 2006.

Robertson, Stacey M. *Parker Pillsbury: Radical Abolitionist, Male Feminist*. Ithaca, NY: Cornell University Press, 2000.

Singleton, William Henry. *Recollections of My Slavery Days*. Peekskill, NY: Highland Democrat Co. Print., 1922. http://docsouth.unc.edu/neh/singleton/singleton.html.

Stauffer, John, and Zoe Trodd, eds. *The Tribunal: Responses to John Brown and the Harpers Ferry Raid*. Cambridge, MA: Belknap Press of Harvard University Press, 2012.

Varon, Elizabeth R. *Appomattox*. New York: Oxford University Press, 2013).

Yacovone, Donald, ed. *A Voice of Thunder: A Black Soldier's Civil War*. Urbana: University of Illinois Press, 1998.

Epilogue

Bay, May. *To Tell the Truth Freely: The Life of Ida B. Wells*. New York: Macmillan, 2010.

Blight, David. *Race and Reunion: The Civil War in American Memory*. Cambridge, MA: Harvard University Press, 2002.

British and Foreign Anti-Slavery Society. "Special Report of the Anti-Slavery Conference held in Paris … in August 1867." London: W. M. Watts, 1867.

Cumbler, John T. *From Abolition to Rights for All*. Philadelphia: University of Pennsylvania Press, 2007.

Douglass, Frederick. "The Lessons of the Hour." Internet Archive: https://archive.org/details/09359080.4757.emory.edu.

DuBois, W. E. B. *The Souls of Black Folk*. Chicago: Dodd, Mead, 1903. http://docsouth.unc.edu/church/duboissouls/menu.html.

Foner, Eric. *Reconstruction: America's Unfinished Revolution, 1863–1877*. New York: HarperPerennial, 2014.

Jeffrey, Julie. *Abolitionists Remember*. Chapel Hill: University of North Carolina Press, 2008.

Abolitionism

Keith, LeeAnna. *The Colfax Massacre: The Untold Story of Black Power, White Terror, and the Death of Reconstruction*. New York: Oxford University Press, 2009.

Nabuco, Joaquim. *O Abolcionismo*. São Paolo: Publifolha, 2003.

"Proceedings of the National Conference of Colored Men of the United States…held at Nashville, Tennessee." Washington, DC: R. H. Darby, 1879.

Schmidt-Nowara,Christopher. *Slavery, Freedom and Abolition in Latin America and the Atlantic World*. Albuquerque: University of New Mexico Press, 2011.

Smith, John David, ed. *A Just and Lasting Peace: A Documentary History of Reconstruction*. New York: Signet, 2013.

Further reading

Websites

The United States/North America:

The Abolition Seminar (The Library Company of Philadelphia):
http://www.abolitionseminar.org

The Black Abolitionist Archive (University of Detroit-Mercy):
http://research.udmercy.edu/find/special_collections/
digital/baa/

The Liberator: Internet Archive: https://archive.org/details/
liberator1831garr

North American Slave Narratives (University of North Carolina):
http://docsouth.unc.edu/neh/

Samuel J. May Anti-Slavery Collection (Cornell University):
http://dlxs.library.cornell.edu/m/mayantislavery/

Great Britain/The Caribbean:

The Black Presence (UK National Archives): http://www.
nationalarchives.gov.uk/pathways/blackhistory/index.htm

The Campaign for Abolition: http://www.bl.uk/learning/histcitizen/
campaignforabolition/abolition.html

Haiti:

American Slavery Debate: Documents on Revolution and Abolition
in Haiti (Stanford University): https://atlanticslaverydebate.
stanford.edu/module3_documents_collection

Latin America:

Slavery, Freedom and Abolition in Latin America: Primary Sources and Online and Selected Archives (Yale University): https://guides.library.yale.edu/c.php?g=296376&p=1977038

Documentaries

Africans in America (Boston: WGBH Productions, 1996).

Britain's Forgotten Slave Owners (London: BBC, 2017).

Egalité for All: Toussaint Louverture and the Haitian Revolution (Washington, DC: PBS Video, 2009).

Slavery and the Making of America (New York: WNET Productions, 2004).

The Abolitionists (Boston: WGBH Productions, 2013).

Underground Railroad: The William Still Story (Buffalo, NY: WNED Productions, 2012).

Index

Index

Index

Index

Index